lonely planet

BEST in TRAVEL

2025

The Best Destinations, Journeys & Experiences for the Year Ahead

CONTENTS

TOP 10
Countries

TOP 10
Cities

TOP 10
Regions

TOP 10
Travel Trends

1 Fiji's remote and reef-fringed Yasawa Islands 2 Coast-hop from Genoa to Ligurian highlights like the Cinque Terre's Manarola 3 Heady views from the Bavarian Alps' Zugspitze, Germany 4 Know where to go birdwatching for a chance to see the majestic great horned owl

INTRODUCTION

by Tom Hall

At Lonely Planet, we love to travel as much as you do. And if there's one thing better than setting out on a trip, it's the anticipation of doing so – the planning, the debating the ins and outs of a trip, the packing. But it all starts with that simple question: where?

maybe the history, nature and wild seashore of the US state of Georgia, which completes our headline attractions.

Those are just the start though. Hopefully *Best in Travel 2025* has something to inspire everyone, whether you're exploring the historical and culinary treasures of Palma de Mallorca, hiking through olive groves and silent wadis on the Jordan Trail or discovering little-known Laos. Passionate pitches from our writers compelled the inclusion of the seaside bohemia of India's Puducherry (Pondicherry), Pacific adventure hotspot Vanuatu and the gentler charms of East Anglia at the green edge of England.

Making *Best in Travel* has been an annual celebration of everything we love about travel for the fifteen years we've published the book. This longevity means the process of pulling these suggestions together is one of the highlights of life at Lonely Planet. First we ask our contributors – an ever-increasing number of whom are locally based experts around the world – for their ideas. Then we have those suggestions independently voted for and ranked. In a world of artificial intelligence, *Best in Travel* remains a deliberate compilation of human experience. We're excited to give these recommendations because we've been to these places ourselves.

Best in Travel, then, aims to solve the 'where' of travel in 2025. What about the 'what'? This year we've also included some lighthearted inspiration that didn't fit into any one place in particular, reflecting travel trends that Lonely Planet has covered in print and online. Taking a trip to see a favourite musical act or tasting what's cooked up in

Perhaps the book you're holding in your hands is the first step in answering that question. 2025 could be the year to visit the volcanoes, rainforests and beaches of Cameroon, our top country. Or Toulouse, France's coral-coloured, culture-rich metropolis, which heads our city list. Or

1 Stunning Haukland Beach, in Norway's Lofoten Islands 2 Wadi Rum moonscape, Jordan Trail 3 Bavaria's Neuschwanstein Castle, Germany 4 Neon nights in Osaka, Japan 5 Jungle-swathed Wat Pha Lat Temple in Chiang Mai, Thailand 6 Sunset over the High Tatras, Slovakia

5

that city or even at one particular establishment are simply superb excuses to visit somewhere new at the same time. Happily, there's also enthusiasm for travelling in as low-impact a way as possible – 10 fresh train-hopping suggestions await for flight-free fun. How about making a pilgrimage to find one very special tree, plunging through the undergrowth in search of an unusual Bird of Paradise, or seeing how the drag scene is wowing crowds in unexpected places – all of these are fast-emerging trends that make for the best stories on returning home.

It feels important to recognise that everyone who travels for the simple joy of doing so enjoys great fortune. The collection of ideas and suggestions for *Best in Travel 2025* took place against a backdrop of instability and conflict in many parts of the world, some new, some very old. There are too many countries Lonely Planet cannot safely cover or recommend visiting where, more importantly, travel is a one-way route out for innocent people living there.

If you're reading this though, decisions may remain simpler. So perhaps *Best in Travel* answers the basics: 'where' and 'what'. From there, a year of adventures awaits. Let the anticipation begin.

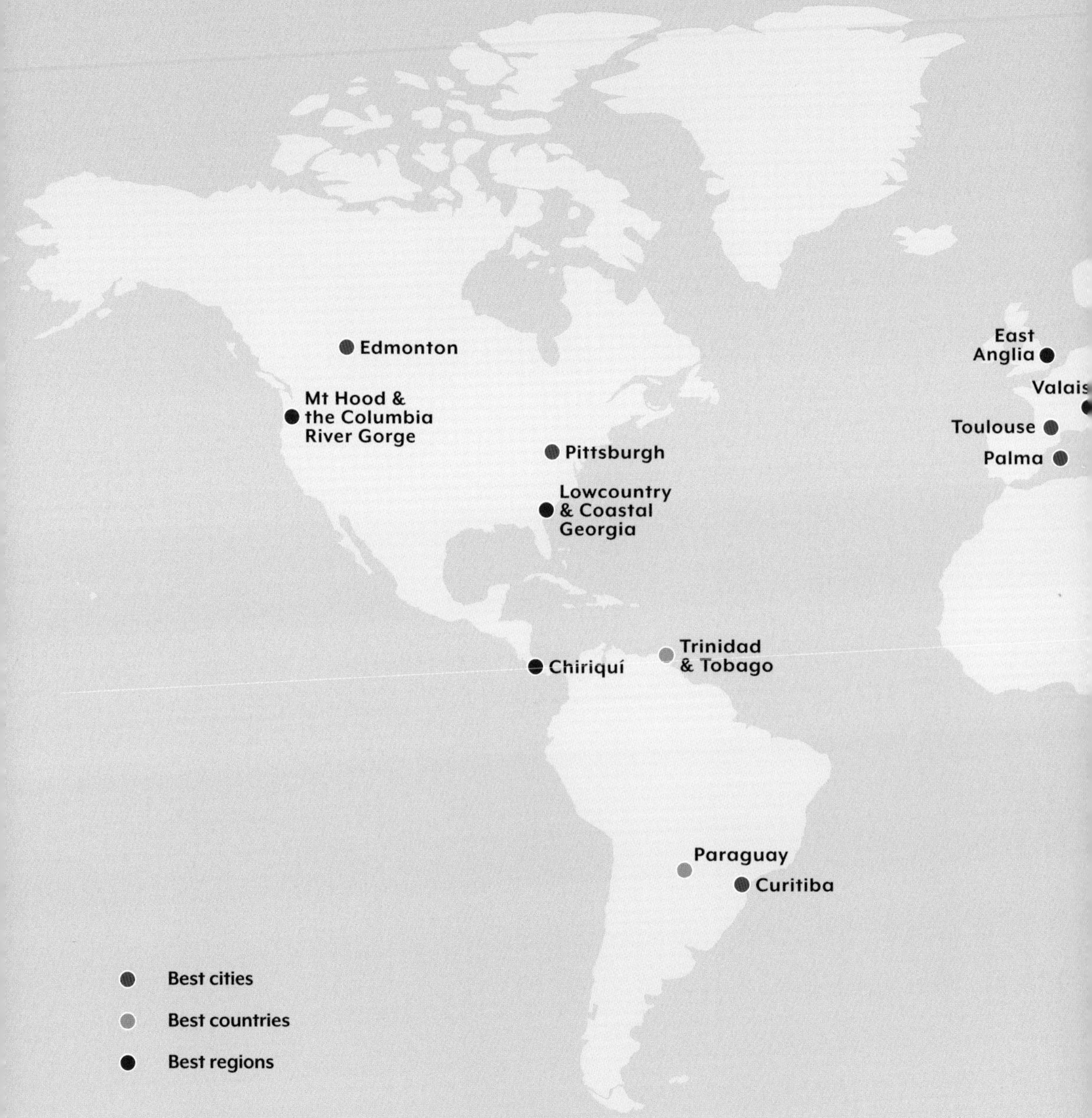

Edmonton

Mt Hood &
the Columbia
River Gorge

Pittsburgh

Lowcountry
& Coastal
Georgia

East
Anglia

Valais

Toulouse

Palma

Trinidad
& Tobago

Chiriquí

Paraguay

Curitiba

- Best cities
- Best countries
- Best regions

Lithuania

Bavaria
Slovakia

Genoa

Giresun
& Ordu

Bansko

Armenia

Kazakhstan

Osaka

Jordan
Trail

Terai

Chiang Mai

Laos

Puducherry

Cameroon

Vanuatu

Fiji

Launceston
& the Tamar
Valley

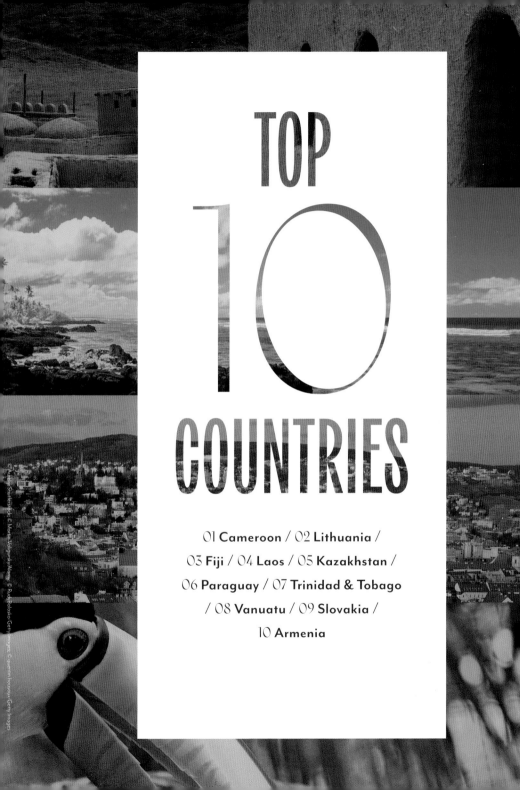

TOP 10 COUNTRIES

© Arsliso Shutterstock; © Maria Vazquez/Alamy; © Rudi Balasko/Getty Images; © quentin houyoux/Getty Images

01

Cameroon

highlights

1 / Shop for flamboyant bronze and beaded crafts at **Village des Artisans** in the attractive town of Foumban.

2 / Enjoy utterly lovely **Kribi** and its beautiful palm trees, waterfalls, white sands and fishing villages.

3 / Head to capital **Yaoundé** to check out Art Deco and Independence architecture as well as esoteric museums.

4 / Go looking for mandrills, gorillas and forest elephants in **Parc National de Campo Ma'an** – after saving sea turtles on the beach at nearby Ebodjé.

C ameroon, celebrating the 65th anniversary of its independence in 2025, is a country on the move, an evolving tide of music and traditional culture that's a whole lot of fun to swim in. From chocolate-coloured beaches and West Africa's highest mountain to exuberant cities and vast tracts of wilderness, Cameroon invites full-scale immersion. Despite a simmering crisis in the north-west and some no-go areas in the north, most of the country is enjoying its role as the continent's next adventure destination.

EMPTY BEACHES

You've seen the headlines: Africa and its safaris are seeing unprecedented popularity, very often to the detriment of the experience.

Let's start with the coast. Countries that have beaches like Cameroon's can only fly under the radar for so long. At a time when travellers are looking beyond well-worn trails, for a place that offers something a little different and has yet to be changed by mass tourism, Cameroon more than delivers, with deserted beaches close to where rainforest-clad Mt Cameroon meets a sheltered corner of the Atlantic Ocean. Beyond a handful of comfortable hotels, the coast from Limbe to Ebodjé is pretty empty and all about eating fresh fish beneath the palm trees with your feet in the sand. And what sand. This stretch of the Cameroonian shore does west-facing white-sand beaches as pretty as any in Africa, but around Limbe, many also come in hues of the deepest chocolate, a legacy of lava flows in centuries past. Further south, around Ebodjé, you can join a sea-turtle conservation project. And Kribi could just be Africa's next world-class beach resort in waiting – but for now remains refreshingly untouched. It's all an experience that's difficult to find anywhere else in Africa, but it won't stay like this forever.

NON-STOP CITIES

Cameroon's cities swagger. From steamy Douala to fun, fascinating Yaoundé, the capital, these contrasting metropolises are the African city writ large. Yaoundé in particular is decked in glorious foliage, arrayed across seven hills, its streets lined with 1960s, Independence-era Art Deco architecture, museums, cafes and bars.

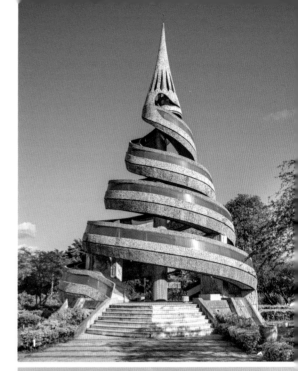

Chutes d'Ekom Nkam, southwest of Foumban 1 The striking Independence-era Monument de la Réunification in central Yaoundé 2 Peaceful, palm-swathed shores around Kribi

> Follow the music. You can't be sad in Yaoundé, where the music never stops. And with music there's always dancing. Take a tour, make a friend, then get them to show you the Yaoundé night.

SAMUEL HAROUNA
/ Tour guide in Yaoundé

In both cities, expect an eclectic soundtrack drawn from the dance-heavy rumba rhythms of central Africa; endless traffic; friendly, confident people; markets bathed in a riot of coloured textiles; masks and wooden statues for sale and so much more. Yaoundé and Douala are going about their business whether the rest of the world knows it or not. And unlike elsewhere, international visitors are few, and very rarely the centre of attention.

THE CALL OF THE WILD
You don't have to stray far beyond city limits to find yourself enveloped in dense woodland of the deepest greens. The huge forests of the Congo Basin extend from the country's interior to its coast – there are times when it can feel as if the whole of Cameroon is one big rainforest. A few national parks provide focal points, from Parc National de Campo Ma'an near Ebodjé in the far south

5

(where the World Wildlife Fund oversees a forest teeming with elephants, primates and leopards) to the remote parks of the country's east, where just getting there is part of the fun. Parks such as these are gaining kudos internationally as conservation success stories, so 2025 may be the last year that you'll have them all to yourself.

3 Hiking between volcanic craters in Parc National du Mont Cameroun, northwest of Douala 4 Down south near Ebodjé, seek out mandrills, gorillas and elephants in the Parc National de Campo Ma'an 5 Tropical fruits in Douala's Grand Marché

when to go

Try to avoid the rainy season (April to October) if you can, when torrential tropical storms sweep down from the Congo Basin; the November-to-February dry season promises the best road and weather conditions.

how to get there

Cameroon lies just off major international routes, but Air France (Paris), Royal Air Maroc (Casablanca) and Ethiopian Airlines (Addis Ababa) all have direct flights into the country.

further reading

Start with *The Overloaded Ark* by Gerald Durrell, *The Poor Christ of Bomba* by Mongo Beti and *Your Madness, Not Mine* by Juliana Makuchi Nfah-Abbenyi. Make sure your playlist is heavy with saxophone legend Manu Dibango.

02
Lithuania

highlights

1 / Toast **Vilnius** after dark with craft cocktails at Champaneria, followed by live music and dancing at party-loving Bardakas.

2 / Cycle and swim in summer, and ice-fish, snow-walk and admire wind-sculpted ice works in winter on the fragile tendril of sand dune protected by the **Curonian Spit National Park**.

3 / Follow pilgrims to the emotive **Hill of Crosses** near Šiauliai, a powerful remembrance site made up of 100,000-plus crosses of all shapes and sizes.

4 / Get lost in ancient oak forests and a labyrinth of wild boating lakes in the untouched **Aukštaitija National Park**.

Europe's last pagan country to be Christianised. Ex-Soviet state shackled by decades of stagnation. Millennial eco-creative. Lithuania is a beguiling destination infused with historical heartache and a fearlessness synonymous with a country that slumbered in the shadows for far too long. In its modern capital, Vilnius, a spirited counterculture offsets an inborn reverence for tradition. As the nation gathers behind its leading lady in its star role as European Green Capital 2025, there's never been a more exciting time to dive into this land of pines, lakes and sand dunes on the Baltic Sea.

A GREEN CITY IN THE MAKING

Nowhere is Lithuania's intrinsically feisty soul more explicit than in its bold and beautiful Baroque capital, Vilnius, a city that places its inhabitants firmly first – 'happiness', 'long lifespan' and 'short commutes' were top criteria in its winning pitch to the European Commission for the Green

Capital accolade. Cycling lanes ribbon through this delightfully compact city to join the dots between leafy parks, the occasional 17th-century ducal palace (such as the recently restored Sapieha Palace, now a contemporary arts centre) and a UNESCO-prized Old Town crafted from cobbled alleys, churches and a summertime abundance of enchanting cafe terraces. Green spaces cover 61% of the capital; a 100km (60 miles) cycling and running trail loops around it; and public-sharing bikes, scooters and cars encourage urbanites to reduce their carbon count. By 2026 there'll also be 16 hydrogen-powered city buses, followed, by 2030, with fossil fuel alternatives powering 80% of public transport.

Once nicknamed the 'Jerusalem of the north', Vilnius' Jewish district was largely destroyed during WWII. A new Museum of Culture and Identity of Lithuanian Jews, in the former ghetto library on Pylimo St, celebrates the country's Jewish heritage and the part it played in the country's rich and diverse DNA. Noble laureates Aaron Klug and Bernard Lown, and artists Jacques Lipchitz and Mark Antokolski, top the museum's emotive roll call of Lithuanian Jewish alumni.

Meandering this highly walkable city, from the stately neoclassical cathedral to artsy Užupis or the newly regenerated Paupys neighbourhood, heart-wrenching reminders of loss loom large: Holocaust memorials, former ghettos, preserved KGB

Vilnius in its autumnal glory 1 Cafe culture in the capital's Paupys district 2 The freestanding belfry of Vilnius Cathedral, framed by the neoclassical columns fronting the main building

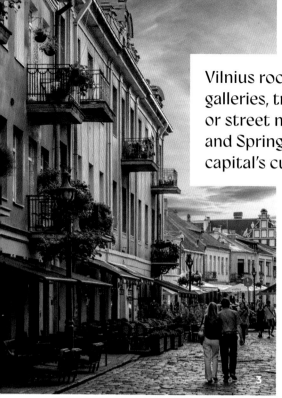

Vilnius rocks with creativity, be it fine art galleries, trees dressed in knitting, local crafts or street musicians. Its Street Music Festival and Spring Film Festival are the jewels on the capital's cultural calendar crown.

EGLĖ NUTAUTAITĖ
/ Lithuanian novelist

torture chambers, graveyards filled with war dead, like the sea of stones in Antakalnis' hauntingly beautiful cemetery. Occasionally, dark places are flipped on their head with style and edge. Where can you sweat it out like a hardened Balt in a traditional sauna, hobnob with local creators and artists, and dance until dawn in a 19th-century jail where prisoners were incarcerated until 2019? At experimental arts venue Lukiškės Prison 2.0 in Vilnius, that's where.

BACK TO NATURE

Lithuania has an otherworldly quality. Thank the Baltic Sea breeze or midsummer's intoxicating white nights, when the sun scarcely sets and night owls fuel up on vodka, craft beer and medieval *midus* (mead). Comb beaches for crumbs of golden amber around Klaipėda. Chill out with ice fishers on Nida's bewitching frozen lagoon. Forest-bathe in woodlands alive with wild elks and sculpted pagan gods in eastern and southern Lithuania. Forage for wild berries and float in island-freckled lakes in the pristine Aukštaitija and Dzūkija National Parks. And lose yourself in the whispering rushes and perfect serenity of the Nemunas Delta birding paradise.

3 © Angel Villalba/Getty Images 4 © A. Aleksandravicius/Shutterstock 5 A. Aleksandravicius/Shutterstock

5

Whatever the outdoor adventure, the uplifting pulse of the seasons and rhythms of the land are exhilarating. Five national parks and 30 regional parks protect 18.3% of the country, with new hiking trails and treetop observation decks popping up everywhere. In 2025, at the prestigious Venice Architecture Biennale, Lithuania's entry celebrates indigenous 'Tree Architecture' and raises awareness of greenwashing by contemporary architects. Yes, traditional woodcarving, harking back centuries in Lithuania, never went out of style.

3 Vilnius' charmingly cobblestoned Old Town **4** From mighty to mini, some 100,000 crucifixes adorn the Hill of Crosses remembrance site near Šiauliai **5** Hiking the peaceful pine forests of Curonian Spit National Park

when to go

June to August ushers in long sunny days, short nights, a warmer Baltic Sea and a bonanza of cultural festivals. It scarcely gets dark around midsummer in late June.

how to get there

International flights land at Vilnius and Kaunas airports, and excellent rail links with Warsaw make light work of training it to/from other European cities. Ferries sail to Klaipėda from Kiel (Germany) and Karlshamn (Sweden).

further reading

Dig into Lithuania's modern soul with two spellbinding novels: *Asphalt Kids* by Eglė Nutautaitė; and *The Last Girl* by Stephan Collishaw, set in Vilnius during WWII and the 1990s.

03

Fiji

PACIFIC
OCEAN

Lambasa

Savusavu

Lautoka

Levuka

Suva

highlights

1 / Experience the unity of a **kava ceremony** while bonding over the ritualistic sharing of a communal bowl.

2 / Scuba dive or snorkel Fiji's **protected marine areas** to explore its coral reefs and warm tropical waters.

3 / Enjoy Fijian culture and hospitality through a cultural experience such as those offered by the sustainable tourism collective **Duavata**.

4 / Head to the country's **highlands and waterfalls** for an authentic jungle and nature encounter.

Against the gentle rhythm of Lali drums and lapping waves, Fiji unfolds across over 330 palm-fringed islands, each a symphony of turquoise waters, vibrant coral reefs and pearl-hued beaches. From the highlands to the high tide, Fijians take immense pride in their homeland and revel in the opportunity to share its beauty and culture with travellers. With open arms and the heartfelt greeting of 'Bula!', Fiji offers more than a slice of paradise – it's a genuine invitation to be part of boundless charm and an appealing mix of culture, nature and hospitality.

SAFEGUARDING THE SEA

Divers and snorkellers swim in awe through Fiji's expansive marine realm, covering 3.4 million sq km (1.3 million sq miles) of cerulean waters and boasting over 460 protected marine areas brimming with biodiversity. Within this aquatic wonderland, more than 1200 species of reef fish dart among the 390 distinct types of coral, while the waters are patrolled by an astonishing variety of over 75 shark and ray species. These natural treasures are pillars of Fiji's cultural heritage and economic vitality, particularly for the tourism sector – and 2025 will see the growth of conservation endeavours aiming to safeguard, rejuvenate and actively engage visitors on a voyage of stewardship in this precious oceanic environment.

Tourism Fiji hopes to transform traditional holiday indulgence into a more meaningful pursuit. A new destination-wide initiative invites travellers to dedicate an hour each day to Fiji's preservation through engaging activities such as planting coral and mangroves – reflecting the philosophy that true happiness stems from generosity. Tourism Fiji and the Professional Association of Diving Instructors (PADI) have joined forces to launch the Bula Blue scheme, a forward-thinking project with a vision to position the country as a leader in sustainable travel. This collaboration is set to establish an extensive network of PADI Eco Center dive shops with a core mission of conservation and sustainability. The scheme is designed to foster regenerative tourism that enriches Fiji's local communities too.

Ambitiously aiming to expand Marine Protected Areas by 30% by the year 2030, Bula Blue also plans to implement the Adopt the Blue programme, a community-driven effort focused on reef conservation across all Fijian dive sites. Additionally, Padi Aware is set to play a pivotal role in bolstering these endeavours by providing locals with career opportunities in diving, thereby deepening

The emerald-swathed isles and reef-rich waters of the Yasawa Group 1 Idyllic island hideaways in the Mamanuca Group 2 Middle Tavoro Waterfalls in Bouma National Heritage Park on Taveuni, Fiji's jungle-swathed 'Garden Island'

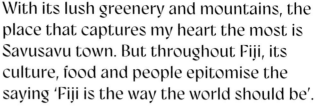

With its lush greenery and mountains, the place that captures my heart the most is Savusavu town. But throughout Fiji, its culture, food and people epitomise the saying 'Fiji is the way the world should be'.

KITTY WEATHERALL
/ Manager, Jean-Michel Cousteau Resort

their connection to and stewardship of the marine environment. Manta Project Fiji, working with the Manta Trust and resorts like Kokomo Private Island and Barefoot Manta, promotes manta ray conservation through research, tagging and responsible snorkelling with these elegant giants, along with Adopt a Manta programmes. Similarly, Beqa Adventure Divers elevates conservation with its Fiji Shark Lab, a research hub for shark and ray preservation which is funded by dive shop revenue, their world-famous shark dives and a shark adoption initiative.

CULTURAL EXPERIENCES

Fiji's allure extends beyond its gleaming shores and biodiverse waters. A country that's rated one of the happiest nations in the world, it's clear from the moment you arrive that the true essence of this place shines through its people. Fijians extend an invitation to experience their cultural tapestry, expressed in exuberant dances and heartfelt melodies that will see you immersed in the communal spirit of a *kava* ceremony sooner than you think. The tourism industry embraces its culture in a way that doesn't feel insincere or contrived. Teams at Nanuku

3 © peacefoo/Shutterstock 4 © Feverpitched/Getty Images 5 © J S. Lamy/Shutterstock

5

Resort, Turtle Island and Jean-Michel Cousteau Resort ensure local traditions and culture are respected and play an active part in the guest experience, while activities like Talanoa Treks, Namosi Eco Retreat and Domoika Adventures – all of which are under the sustainable tourism collective Duavata – engage visitors with traditional Fijian culture through adventure.

3 Locally grown produce at the market in Nadi, on Fiji's west coast 4 The rainbow-hued collared lory parrot, just one of the distinctive endemic bird species that flit through the islands' rainforests 5 A kaleidoscope of colours on a Fijian reef

when to go

Experience Fiji's pearl-hued beaches in the monsoon months from November to April, enjoying affordable rates and solitude between rain showers. The rest of the year offers abundant sun but larger crowds.

how to get there

Fiji Airways has convenient direct flights from North America, Asia, Australia and New Zealand, and seamless connections to Europe with partner airlines.

04

Laos

highlights

1 / Visit Vientiane's **Pha That Luang temple** and **Patuxay**, a recreation of France's Arc de Triomphe that's a reminder of Laos' colonial past.

2 / Disembark at **Luang Prabang** for day trips to Kuang Si Waterfall and the Old Quarter, and to join the sunrise alms-giving ceremony on Sisavangvong Rd.

3 / Stroll the **Golden Temple Scenic Area**, just outside Kunming, to explore its religious spaces, forest park, botanical garden and open-air museum.

4 / See the **Dynamic Yunnan performance** at Yunnan Yingxiang Theatre, a grand and unique musical that depicts the history and lives of ethnic minorities in Southwest China.

Southeast Asia is famed for its slow, ageing rail systems that garner much attention from laid-back travellers and video bloggers alike. Yet while its neighbours plod along with little changing since the 1970s, Laos has opened a brand-new, high-speed international rail network that connects the country's quiet mountainous plains with China's bustling southwestern Yunnan Province. This 'Trans-Asian' express gives the old and hard-to-access Trans-Siberian a run for its money, with comfortable trains, cheap tickets, subtropical climes and a wealth of must-see landmarks along its tracks.

THE CHINA–LAOS RAILWAY ADVENTURE

Given Southeast Asia's long-lasting appeal for travellers and backpackers, the trend towards lesser-trodden-path adventures has left the region feeling a little uncertain of its future popularity. Lucky, this new engineering marvel, connecting the region to the vast and epic landscapes of southern China, may just be the next bucket-list trip to keep the area front of mind.

The China–Laos Railway's 1035km (643 miles) are far more than just a rail trip. It's a hop-on hop-off network that connects some of Asia's best, yet relatively unseen, cultural and natural wonders. This route is an essential experience for those looking to beat the crowds and earn 'before it was cool' bragging rights prior to the line's planned extension through Thailand, Malaysia and Singapore.

Aside from all the sustainable benefits that come with train travel, the cosy carriages and convenient schedules also make this a great choice for those seeking an authentic, on-the-ground adventure.

KINDRED CAPITALS

Whether you board in Yunnan and head south or grab a ticket in the Laotian capital of Vientiane, the silky-smooth high-speed train offers some of the region's best views, speeding past towering mountains, vast rice paddies and enchanting Chinese cities that echo a quieter side of Asia less visited by foreign tourists. Each stop is a world of its own. The end-of-the-line cities could not be any more different in appearance, but in spirit they are kindred. Vientiane in Laos is a truly unique place that balances tradition with modernity under Buddhist–Communist rule. Kunming shares a similar laid-back and peaceful vibe that still feels more Southeast

Hilltop living near Luang Namtha 1 Vientiane's Arc de Triomphe replica, Patuxai commemorates the Lao who died in prerevolutionary wars 2 The gilded Wat Ho Pha Bang, home to the Buddha image from which Luang Prabang takes its name

> Before the train, buses between the main towns could take all day. Now it's an hour or less, which means more time to explore.

CHRIS SCHALKX
/ Journalist

Asia than China. It's known locally as the 'Spring City' due to a temperate year-round climate that pairs well with a collection of naturally beautiful landmarks, well-maintained public spaces, hot springs, lakes and museums.

LITTLE-KNOWN SIGHTS IN THE BLINK OF AN EYE

Travelling at 160kp/h (100mph), the Vientiane–Boten portion of the route navigates 162 bridges (two that span the Mekong River and measure over a kilometre each) and 72 tunnels interspersed with verdant landscapes and untouched mountains. The train's path also reveals some of the country's lesser-seen but incredibly beautiful ancient towns such as Luang Prabang, Oudomxay and Luang Namtha. All worthy of an overnight stopover if you have the time.

Boten in Laos or Mohan in China is where you pass through immigration before crossing the border. Coming from Laos, you'll enter the Xishuangbanna Autonomous Prefecture of Southern China, eventually passing through Yuxi, Pu'er and Kunming South before finally arriving at the Yunnanese capital. This section is made up of two lines, slowing on entry to Yunnan some 90km (56 miles) out from the terminal station.

5

From end to end, the trip takes around 10 and a half hours, including time at customs and immigration. Previously, the only connection between the two was by the Kunming–Vientiane bus that took over 22 hours. Budget travellers can revel in the surprising news that the train and bus have very similar ticket prices, while those wanting to avoid the crowds should see 2025 as the year to go before it becomes overwhelmed with the busy backpacker crowd.

3 The Edenic waterfalls of Kuang Si, an easy day trip from Luang Prabang 4 Barbecued fish on a Laotian street-food stall 5 Walking through the rain showers in Luang Prabang

how to get there

Booking tickets for the China–Laos Railway requires different methods for each section. In China, tickets can be pre-booked via the official website www.12306.cn or at train station ticket agents at every stop. In Laos, as online booking is not available yet, tickets must be purchased from stations or agents, with a pre-booking period of just three days. Tickets are very affordable, but prices can vary based on demand, season and timing. First-class seats generally go for around CNY850 ($120) while second-class seats range from CNY200-600 ($30-85). There are no sleeper berths.

05

Kazakhstan

RUSSIA

Astana
Nauruyz celebration
Aqtobe
Qaraghandy

CHINA

Bozjyra Restaurant

Altyn-Emel National Park
Almaty
Auyl Restaurant

UZBEKISTAN
Shymkent

KYRGYZSTAN

TURKMENISTAN

Kazakhstan is not just a place to visit; it's a world to enter, a journey to undertake and a story to become a part of, with ghosts from the Silk Road whispering across the vast steppes that surround Kazakhstan's cities. Make cosmopolitan Almaty your starting point for a Kazakh adventure, and then roam the rough, wild mountains and steppe, visiting Soviet space centres and ancient trading towns as you cross this country still uncrowded by tourists.

TO THE EAST

'Trains in these parts went from East to West, and from West to East' – take inspiration from the words of Chinghiz Aitmatov, one of Central Asia's most influential authors, and travel Kazakhstan by train.

Almaty, the old capital, is cradled by mountains and holds the essence of Kazakhstan's Soviet heritage within its neighbourhoods, known as microdistricts. Walk through

highlights

1 / Dine at **Auyl**, outside Almaty, where design, history and neo-nomad cuisine meet.

2 / Visit the 3km (2 miles) singing dunes in **Altyn-Emel National Park** and hear the organ-like hum emitted from the sands and the wind.

3 / Try *beshbarmak*, a celebratory dish made with horse or mutton at restaurant **Bozjyra** in Shymkent.

4 / Join three days of festivities during **Nauruyz** (aka Nowruz), the Persian first day of spring – every city and village has feasts, dances and traditional games, but Astana is the top pick.

the bustling Green Bazaar, marvel at the intricate architecture of Zenkov Cathedral and listen to the call to prayer from the minarets of the Central Mosque. Outside Almaty, you can get back in touch with nature. Hop in a 4WD and visit Charyn Canyon to inspect its 12-million-year-old rock formations. Then be transported to dense forest by driving down to Kolsai Lakes National Park. For those drawn to the enigmatic, the *barkhan*, aka the singing dunes, in Altyn-Emel National Park, offer an otherworldly symphony of nature's own making.

The capital city of Astana is known for its ultra-modern, shiny architecture, but there's a cultural side too, seen in visits to the theatre, the National Museum or the poet Saken Seifullin's former home.

Saddle up in the wilds of Katon-Karagay National Park, in the country's far east, to explore the lush valleys and mountains near the Russian and Mongolian borders on horseback. In 2021, a camera trap showed that the rare snow leopard still calls the park home.

IN BETWEEN

Visit the Soviet side of the space race at the Baikonur Cosmodrome (permit required), still in action today. In advance, space buffs can reserve a 5-day tour leading up to launch day – there are about four per year.

Nomadic shepherds and their revered Kazakh horses make camp on the mountain-fringed steppes **1** Hunting with trained golden eagles near Almaty **2** Hiking through the ancient rock columns of Charyn Canyon

> Almaty to me means mountain peaks that surround the city. Surrounded by Tian Shan spruce trees, on horseback or on foot, there is nowhere else I feel like going any time of year.

ANELY NAZARBEK
/ Almaty outdoors enthusiast

In the south, near the border with Uzbekistan, Shymkent is an ancient caravan crossroads and Kazakhstan's third-largest city today, known for some of the country's best food. Check out the street art on Suleymenova St, or in April and May head to the mountains south of the city when they're covered in tulips – drive out for a day of *chachlyk* (kebabs) and fresh air. Hikers will love the many trails in the Sairam-Ugam National Park, and might wake up with wild animals like deer grazing outside their tents.

Hop back on the train to reach Turkestan, a city with strong Sufi heritage. Attracting many pilgrims, its mosques and mausoleums are similar in style to the Silk Road cities of Samarkand and Bukhara in Uzbekistan.

TO THE WEST

Venture to the edge of the Caspian Sea where the city of Aktau is a curious place; sandy, with the odour of gas in the air, it is flanked by the desolate badlands. Wander along the seashore, eye up the local street style, and eat where the locals eat, in the garden of the Caravan restaurant. The most interesting site near Aktau is the Ustyurt

3 © Cavan Images/Getty Images   4 © Hihtellin/Shutterstock   5 © Pikoso.kz/Shutterstock

5

Reserve, where deep into the deserted steppe lie pillars of limestone and chalk in pinks, blues and whites, reaching hundreds of metres into the air. Spot herds of Kazakh saiga antelope, Persian gazelles and evasive mouflons. Today, all that's left of the once busy Silk Road stopover the ruins of Shakhr-i-Vazir, the Beleuli *caravanserai* and the Allan fortress, plus mausoleums and underground mosques.

3 Glacial Big Almaty Lake under the snowcapped peaks of the Tien Shan range 4 Traditional Kazakh cuisine 5 Tsarist-era Zenkov, Almaty's candy coloured Russian Orthodox cathedral

when to go

Spring and autumn in the cities and valleys, and summer in the mountains. Winters are harsh but the Altaï range is great for back-country skiing adventures.

how to get there

By plane into Almaty, or by ferry from Baku to Aktau. The country's cities are well connected by rail; the Soviets built a rail system that connects neighbouring countries as well: Russia, Kyrgyzstan and Uzbekistan are all a train ticket away.

06

Paraguay

BOLIVIA

BRAZIL

Pantanal

Pedro Juan
Caballero

Concepción

ARGENTINA

Superclásico

Asunción

Óga Restaurant

Ciudad
del Este

**Carmen
del Paraná**

Jesuit ruins

highlights

1 / Sample **new Paraguayan cuisine** at Óga in Asunción, including catfish sashimi, rib-eye steak, sweet potato purée and yerba mate ice cream.

2 / Sunbathe on the golden beaches of **Carmen del Paraná**.

3 / Voyage upriver to the **Pantanal**, the world's largest tropical wetland, aboard the Siete Cabrillas floating hotel from Concepción.

4 / Stroll among the **Jesuit ruins** of Trinidad, Jesús de Tavarangué and San Cosme y Damián.

5 / Pogo with chanting football fans at the **Superclásico showdown** between top clubs Olimpia and Cerro Porteño.

Hidden in the heart of South America, Paraguay brims with biodiversity and a laid-back, welcoming vibe. There's plenty to reward adventurous travellers, from the spiky Chaco forest – roamed by jaguars and giant anteaters – to picturesque pueblos and plunging waterfalls. Meanwhile, new tours are show-casing the eclectic architecture of Asunción, the charmingly time-worn capital. Less well-trodden than nearby Brazil and Argentina, visitors often have Paraguay's natural and cultural highlights all to themselves. Come before the crowds get here: the country is jointly hosting the 2030 World Cup.

TOUR THE MOTHER OF CITIES

Asunción's roots go back way past the Spanish conquistadors. Its pre-Columbian heritage is palpable: from the Guaraní spoken by shoeshiners to the vendors selling *tereré*, chilled yerba mate with medicinal herbs. It's also embodied in new restaurants championing native ingredients. Táva opened downtown in 2024, offering soul food like *sopa paraguaya* (a cheesy, spongy cornbread) and inventive fusions like *mbeju*, a crispy cassava cake topped with fried egg, beef and kimchi. Chacatours, a local-owned initiative, take visitors into La Chacarita – a historic riverside neighborhood with a rough reputation – and is soon to offer homestays. Once a month, the crumbling turn-of-the-century mansions along Calle Palma open their doors to visitors: you could almost be in Havana. Meanwhile, a craft beer revolution gathers pace. Head to the buzzy patio at Koggi to sample lagers by Herken, no-frills tap room The Hop for *weissbier* and IPAs, or the sleek brewpub Simón Dice for red ales, porters and Kölsch. In 2025, the rebuilding of the long-defunct train line from near the grand old train terminus downtown to the city's outskirts is set to begin in earnest – but don't expect to ride the rails for a while yet.

MAKE TRACKS IN THE CHACO

Barely a mile across the river begins the Great South American Chaco, a tapestry of swamp, savannah and scrub the size of Afghanistan, described by Sir David Attenborough as one of Earth's last great wildernesses. But the Chaco has long been inhabited by over a dozen Indigenous peoples – skilled artisans and careful stewards of their fragile forest home – while recent bridges and roads are making the region more accessible to outsiders. Comfortable hotels can be found in the

The alluring cascades of Saltos del Monday **1** Asunción's eclectic skyline **2** Giant waterlilies bloom on Paraguay's Pantanal wetlands

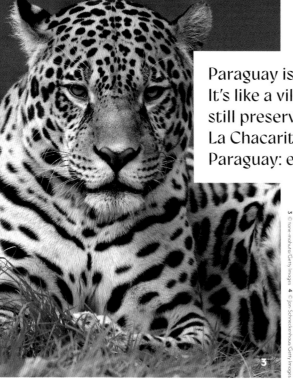

3 © fane mahuta/Getty Images 4 © Jon Schreckenhaus/Getty Images

> Paraguay is waiting to be discovered. It's like a village, stopped in time, where we still preserve a sense of communal living. La Chacarita is the essence, the genesis of Paraguay: everything started there.

CHRISTIAN NUÑEZ
/ Founder, Chacatours

Mennonite town of Filadelfia, seven hours from Asunción. A landmark US$2.3bn visitor centre opened here in 2020, complete with hiking trails and exhibits on the extraordinary flora (sturdy *quebracho* hardwoods, the thorny, bottle-trunked *palo borracho*) and fauna (jaguars, tapirs, flamingos, giant armadillos). Nearby Laguna Capitán is a good place to spot some. Further north lies the majestic Parque Nacional Defensores del Chaco. Tread lightly and visit only with an experienced guide – small groups of Ayoreo hunter-gatherers, the last isolated peoples in the Americas outside the Amazon, live here.

GO CHASING WATERFALLS

Iguazú Falls – just over the border with Argentina and Brazil – hogs the limelight, but Paraguay's eastern region has dozens of other impressive cascades offering adventure tourism, wildlife-spotting and tiny villages frozen in time. Rappel down Salto Cristal – a sheet of glassy spray over dark rock – and camp near the shore amid dense rainforest. Feeding a pool with a view, Salto Inglés is named after the British railwaymen who ran pipes downhill to fill

TOP FIVE
Paraguayan Festivals

1 / **Easter Weekend:** Good Friday procession along Tañarandy's candlelit lanes before Mass at a giant altarpiece of vegetable gourds.

2 / **San Juan Ára:** Midwinter weekends in June are lit up by flaming football games and papier-mache bulls.

3 / **Día de la Independencia:** Paraguay celebrates its independence on 14 and 15 May with harp music and bottle dancers.

4 / **Fiesta de San Blas:** On 3 February, La Chacarita residents carry a statue of Saint Blaise, patron of Paraguay, and crown the *rey de los feos* (King of the Uglies).

5 / **Arete Guasú:** In late February, Indigenous peoples gather to drink maize beer and dance with their ancestors.

4

their locomotives, still lovingly preserved in the town of Sapucai. Salto Samakua tumbles for 60m (197ft) over a cliff: hire a guide in Capitán Bado to find it. Close by the budget shopping malls of Ciudad del Este, the churning Saltos del Monday turn the colour of chocolate milk after heavy rains. You'll need a sturdy vehicle and a full tank to reach some of these places, or tag along with JaikuaaPy, whose tours usually leave Asunción Friday night and return late on Sunday.

3 Paraguay's Chaco is home to jaguars, tapirs and much more: get the lowdown at Filadelfia's fabulous visitor centre 4 Paseo La Galería shopping centre, just one face of modern Asunción

when to go

A great time to visit is between June and November, when the lapacho trees explode with pink and yellow flowers and the weather is slightly cooler.

how to get there

Silvio Pettirossi Airport connects to other South American capitals and Madrid. If visiting Iguazú, you can easily cross into Ciudad del Este. The Chaco can be reached via overnight bus from Santa Cruz, Bolivia.

further reading

Dip into *The Paraguay Reader* for history, social commentary and poetry. Lily Tuck's *The News from Paraguay* is set amid a cataclysmic 19th-century war. *I, the Supreme* was penned in exile by the country's greatest writer, Augusto Roa Bastos.

07

Trinidad & Tobago

Scarborough

CARIBBEAN
SEA

Pigeon
Point Beach

Asa Wright
Nature Centre

Kaiso City Pizza ·   · Port-of-Spain

Chaguanas

·Temple
in the Sea

ATLANTIC
OCEAN

San Fernando   Rio Claro

highlights

1 / Go birding, hiking and turtle-watching at the Hadco Experiences **Asa Wright Nature Centre**, a Northern Range estate that welcomes eco-enthusiasts from around the world.

2 / Enjoy Tobago's cerulean-tinted waves with watersports and popular food spots at **Pigeon Point Beach**. Try the delectable curried crab and dumpling at nearby **Miss Trim's**.

3 / Grab Italian pizzas with fresh, locally sourced ingredients, like chadon beni oil and aubergine, at Port of Spain's **Kaiso City Pizza**.

4 / Check out the sacred Hindu pantheon, **Temple in the Sea**, a colourful, octagonal-shaped structure that sits on a causeway in the Gulf of Paria.

T rinidad and Tobago brings much more than the allure of 'sun, sea and sand'. The twin-island republic is a layered prism of history and heritage where 1.3 million people from diverse ethnic, religious and cultural identities live in harmony – and, infamously, party *hard*. At every adventurous turn, culture is the North Star of this southernmost Caribbean gem. From hypnotic rhythms of soca music during the apex of Trinidad Carnival to mouth-watering delicacies that make every visitor a certified 'foodie', Trinidad and Tobago is a wanderlust's utopian dream in living colour.

AN EXPLOSION OF CULTURE

In several festivals across Trinidad and Tobago, every creed and race finds an equal place – and that's not just an ode to the national anthem. Year-round, visitors have the opportunity to explore vibrant worlds that are profoundly shaped by the country's rich amalgamation of cultures, religions and heritage. It's this anthropological blend that fuses together music, fashion and food – uniquely and unapologetically.

Trinidad Carnival is the flagship staple on the country's festival calendar. It's a months-long extravaganza that features steelpan competitions, stick-fighting battles and calypso showdowns for public viewing. This exciting season culminates with wondrous costume parades on the Monday and Tuesday immediately preceding the Catholic observance of Lent. On those two days, tens of thousands of revellers descend on capital Port of Spain's streets and other parts of the country to party to a sonorous soca soundtrack played from large trucks with speakers. Another festival is Hosay, a Muslim Indo-Caribbean commemoration where larger-than-life mausoleums or tombs known as *tadjah* are paraded and carried out to sea for a ritualised final resting place. Phagwah, or Holi, is the Hindu Festival of Colours when patrons gleefully play in bright powdery hues known as *abir* to signify the triumph of good over evil.

WHERE NATURE MATTERS

Beyond the hustle and bustle of the world-class festival scene, sustainable tourism is becoming an increasingly popular draw for 'serene, clean and green' tropical getaways.

Scarlet ibis fly in to roost in the mangroves of Trinidad's Caroni Swamp **1** Leatherback turtle hatchlings make a break for the sea at Grande Riviere, Trinidad **2** Costumed revellers at T&T's unmissable pre-Lenten Carnival, Port of Spain

> In T&T, we have the biggest melting pot of cultures, resulting in the most amazing food. From fancy restaurants to street food, it's all a celebration of who we are.

CHEF BRIGETTE JOSEPH
/ Culinary and hospitality consultant

There has been a renaissance of eco-friendly attractions that have enriched the visitor experience and brought new life to smaller communities.

The coastal village of Grande Riviere has one of the busiest leatherback nesting sites in the world. Locals banded together to form an association to protect them, patrolling the beach at night to guard against poachers, and then began to offer tours. More places to stay have cropped up as a result, and Grande Riviere now has a small, sustainable tourism scene that directly benefits both locals and the visiting turtles.

A DELIGHTFUL FOODIE FANTASY

If you have a certain craving, it's almost guaranteed that Trinidad and Tobago has a variation of that dish to satisfy your needs. With cultural influences from the African, East Asian, French, Spanish, English, Dutch, Chinese and Indigenous communities, the gastronomy scene is as vast as it is flavourful. Restaurants such as Freebird in South Trinidad offer farm-to-

5

table dining experiences with prized local produce, while Tobago's options include Seahorse Inn, where a seafood paradise is paired with soothing waves rolling in on the nearby beach. Conversely, Port of Spain's Ariapita Ave strip has a more casual, on-the-go food scene. With dishes such as Hassan Gyros pitas, generously stuffed with a mix of lamb and chicken, or the national roadside delight known as doubles (curried chickpea sandwich) served by Sauce Team, visitors can indulge in a variety of options around the clock that are easy on the tastebuds and the wallet.

3 Fruit stall in Scarborough, Tobago's seaside capital
4 Head to birding hotspots like Asa Wright Nature Centre to see colourful species such as the purple honeycreeper
5 Picture-perfect Pigeon Point Beach, Tobago

when to go

Like most Caribbean countries, travel to T&T is enjoyable year-round. June to November marks the rainy season period, and though it's meteorologically defined as hurricane season, precipitation is thankfully not intense enough to stop planned island fun. December to June is the dry season.

how to get there

Piarco International Airport is the easily accessible international flight hub on Trinidad; Tobago is accessible by air (ANR Robinson International Airport) or by inter-island ferry.

further reading

One classic body of literary work that comprehensively illustrates the islands' traditions is Eric Williams' *History of the People of Trinidad and Tobago.*

08

Vanuatu

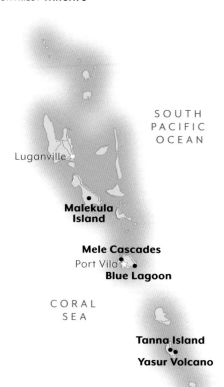

SOUTH
PACIFIC
OCEAN

Luganville

**Malekula
Island**

Mele Cascades
Port Vila
Blue Lagoon

CORAL
SEA

Tanna Island
Yasur Volcano

highlights

1 / Stand on the rim of Tanna Island's **Yasur volcano** as lava spurts into the air.

2 / Sample **Vanuatu's signature beverage**, *kava*, at a local bar on any island.

3 / Scuba dive famous wrecks and coral reefs, or splash around in Efate Island's idyllic **Blue Lagoon** and **Mele Cascades**.

4 / Experience the islands' **rich mix of cultural traditions**, from Tanna Island's quirky John Frum Day festival to the art of sand drawing on Malekula Island, which has its own festival in May.

Magic, mysticism and *kastom* (traditional culture) collide in the wild and rugged 83-island archipelago of Vanuatu, the world's most linguistically diverse nation per capita. Often overlooked by travellers in favour of more developed Pacific Island escapes, Vanuatu's rawness is key to its appeal. Between diving epic wrecks, experiencing ancient rituals and watching lava spew from an active volcano, however, visitors can enjoy an increasing clutch of modern comforts. With a comprehensive national sustainable development plan in action that prioritises the protection of nature for future generations, it's easier to visit with a light footprint, too.

THE HAPPY COUNTRY

The year 2025 marks a decade since one of the worst cyclones to hit the South Pacific devastated Vanuatu. Cyclone Pam wasn't the first severe weather event to hit the country, nor will it be the last, and yet in spite of these hardships this small nation of just 300,000-odd people was recently ranked the world's second happiest country in the Happy Planet Index. It's easier to understand why when you touch down in Port Vila on the main island of Efate. Nestling between a glittering natural harbour and a dreamy turquoise lagoon, Vila is perhaps the world's most idyllically positioned capital. The pace is slow, the welcome is warm, and the setting instantly relaxing. Despite the storms of all kinds weathered by Vanuatu in recent years, there's plenty to be happy about.

ANCIENT LAND, ANCIENT CULTURES

Vanuatu is swathed in jungle, fringed by deserted beaches, dotted with volcanos and laced with scenic trails. But perhaps the most memorable takeaway from a trip here is experiencing the rich and diverse cultures of the Ni-Vanuatu (Melanesian people of Vanuatu, also known as Ni-Van). From the *kastom* tribes of Tanna Island, who continue to maintain a pre-colonial lifestyle in a modern world (and a reverence for the late Duke of Edinburgh), to the captivating Ra Snake Dance performed by the men of Ra Island in the Banks Islands, the opportunities for memorable cultural immersion are endless. But you don't even need to leave Port Vila to sample Ni-Van culture, with *kastom* continuing to play an important role in the daily lives of most locals there too. Port Vila is also the best place to discover the many cultural influences, including French

Kayaking the Matevulu Blue Hole on Espiritu Santo Island
1 Idyllic oceanside accommodation in overwater bungalows
2 Traditional *kastom* dance in the shadow of the Yasur volcano, Tanna Island

> I love shopping for fruits and vegetables at Port Vila Market, as they're organically grown and so fresh. I also often buy some manioc rolls (cassava dough stuffed with meat); they're my favourite!

BEVERLY TEAHIU
/ Local tour guide

and British, which have played a role in shaping everything from Vanuatu's cuisine to the main Bislama language, which evolved during a dark period of Vanuatu's history, when Ni-Van were enslaved by European colonists to labour on plantations in Australia and beyond. This common language now helps to unite a nation home to more than 130 language groups.

TOP FIVE
Dive Sites in Vanuatu

1 / **SS** *President Coolidge:* One of the world's largest and most accessible wreck dives, off Espiritu Santo.

2 / **Tanna Island:** With just one dive centre on the island at White Grass Ocean Resort & Spa, you can enjoy Tanna's two coral-encrusted blue holes by yourself.

3 / **Million Dollar Point:** A graveyard for WWII military equipment in Santo, dumped by the US Navy.

4 / **Owen's Reef:** Off Efate, this vibrant reef contains an enormous diversity of corals.

5 / **Cindy's Reef:** Easily accessible from Santo, this pretty reef is another draw for coral fans.

NEW BEGINNINGS

Vanuatu recently shed its official classification as one of the world's least developed countries – a milestone only a handful of other nations have managed to achieve in the last 40 years. While the lack of development is among its charms, a slew of recent and forthcoming tourism openings and enhancements are set to gently elevate any visit. Closed since the pandemic, the not-for-profit Ratua Private Island Resort in Espiritu Santo Island welcomed guests back to one of Vanuatu's most luxurious and low-impact stays in 2024. Hosting just 42 guests across its 13 restored Javanese villas at any one time, the sea breeze provides the air-con in its 13 villas, and organic island produce features on the menus.

4

5

4 © rob travel/Shutterstock. 5 © Martin Valigursky/Shutterstock.

Recently launched Moso Dream Tours & Transfers offers a new local-owned-and-operated opportunity for adventures in Efate Island, while Tanna Island's White Grass Ocean Resort & Spa, home to the island's only dive centre, has been working with the Vanuatu Fisheries Department to establish a Marine Protected Area designed to safeguard the island's fringing reef and the mesmerising underwater ecosystem it supports.

3 Driftwood sculpture on the Port Vila shore 4 Beachside resort, Efate Island 5 Swim in cool, clear fresh water at Efate's Mele Cascades, near Port Vila

when to go

With just 45,000 tourist arrivals per year, Vanuatu never feels crowded in the high (and dry) season (April to September). Aim to visit Pentecost Island on a Saturday between April and June to take in the ancient Naghol (land diving) ritual that inspired modern bungee jumping; and the Maskelyne Islands in July for the two-day Maskelyne Canoe Race & Arts Festival.

how to get there

There are direct flights to Vanuatu from Australia (Brisbane, Sydney and Melbourne), New Zealand (Auckland), Fiji (Nadi), New Caledonia (Noumea) and Honiara (Solomon Islands).

09

Slovakia

W hen you have famous neighbours like the Czechia and Austria, it's easy to slip under the radar. Bordered by five countries and with rail connections across Europe, Slovakia has long been treated as a swift stopover – if travellers made it here at all. But with revamped historical monuments, renewed emphasis on ecotourism and the rise of its unsung east, Slovakia is poised for travel stardom. This landlocked country of sky-piercing mountains and art-filled towns is now a destination in its own right, thanks to a distinctive architectural medley and well-protected natural beauty.

BRATISLAVA'S BIG MAKEOVER

Slovakia has all the charms you'd expect of Central Europe: Gothic church spires, hilltop castles and quaint galleries. Going into 2025, these cultural riches have never looked better – especially in the capital, Bratislava, where the scaffolding is finally down revealing newly restored landmark

highlights

1/ Admire Brutalist architecture with Bratislava's topsy-turvy **Slovak National Radio Building** or Banská Bystrica's sci-fi domed **Museum of the Slovak National Uprising**.

2/ Go snow-shoeing in the **High Tatras** or scale ladders above thrashing waterfalls in **Slovenský Raj National Park**.

3/ See underground wonders including Europe's largest stalagmite inside **Krásnohorská Cave** and explore the shimmering perma-freeze of **Dobšinská Ice Cave**.

4 / Savour panoramic revolving-restaurant views from Veža inside **Kamzík TV Tower** or dine inside the iconic **UFO building**, both in Bratislava.

buildings. One of these, the Slovak National Gallery, received an award-winning make-over, thoroughly revamping its courtyard and interior galleries, and transforming Dedeček's Bridge – an opinion-dividing 1970s relic within the SNG – into a sleek, light-flooded contemporary space. In the Old Town, Michael's Tower, the only surviving original of Bratislava's four medieval gates, has also been recently restored. And then there's the formerly dilapidated Námestie Slobody (Freedom Square). Its centrepiece, Družba Fountain, was out of action for 16 years, but this blossom-shaped sculpture has finally been repaired. The fountain now flows freely, transforming the square from a local punch-line into a popular meeting place. There are architectural newcomers, too, like the upcoming expansion to Zaha Hadid's residential project Sky Park, and Devínska Kobyla Observation Tower, 11km (7 miles) northwest of Bratislava. This 20m (65ft) lookout, whose shape was inspired by a praying mantis, lets you gaze out at the fields and forests of Slovakia, as well as into neighbouring Austria and Czechia.

THE RISE OF SLOVAK ECOTOURISM

Slovakia has been quietly rising through the green travel ranks, winning sixth place in Euromonitor's 2023 Sustainable Travel Index. The country's nine national parks dazzle with lakes, beech forests and wild-flower meadows that cascade down the flanks of the Carpathian Mountains. Nature

Calm waters at Štrbské Pleso, a High Tatras spa resort
1 St Martin's Cathedral presides over the Bratislava cityscape
2 Spring in the High Tatras sees greening peaks and a bloom of colourful wildflowers

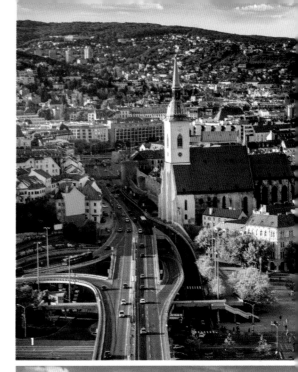

> During the '70s, there were a lot of utopian projects, most of which were never finished. Architecture like Bratislava's UFO building marks the space-race era, where everything was supposed to be possible.

BRANO CHRENKA
/ Co-founder, Authentic Slovakia tours

slumbers undisturbed for six months during the winter closures of most hiking trails in the Tatras, the mountainous spine separating Slovakia from Poland. When hiking season does arrive, you can travel lightly aboard the Tatra Electric Railway, which trundles from lakeside spa town Štrbské Pleso up to mountain resort Tatranská Lomnica. In Bratislava, visit Vydrica Nature Reserve, where moss-cloaked forest is laced with streams. Plans are afoot in the northerly Pieniny region for an eco-friendly tourist trail highlighting 12 natural mineral springs. Meanwhile, in Slovakia's southeastern wine country, tree-top accommodation in Malá Bara offers a unique combination: sipping sweet Tokaj wine while fully surrounded by woodland.

EASTERN SLOVAKIA'S CULTURAL RENAISSANCE

Beyond wine country, eastern Slovakia overflows with offbeat attractions. Eighteen UNESCO sights, from colossal Spiš Castle to tiny 18th-century wooden churches, are within two hours' drive of Košice, the country's easterly second city. Now, there are even more reasons to visit: 30 pieces of street art beautify the city, thanks to the OMG (Open

5

Mural Gallery) project. Košice's creatives are finding a hub in Tabačka Kulturfabrik, a mixed-use venue where bars, concert hall, gallery and co-working spaces meet. Nearby in Košice's city park, a 1909 Art Nouveau building has been rescued from ruin and transformed into five-star Villa Sandy resort. And 110km (68 miles) northeast of Košice, the Andy Warhol Museum of Modern Art in Medzilaborce has been thoroughly over-hauled. Located near the natal village of Warhol's parents, the gallery is slated for a grand reopening at the end of 2024 – just another of the many surprises Slovakia has in store.

3 Bratislava's revamped Slovak National Gallery **4** The cable car up to Lomnický peak from Tatranská Lomnica **5** Combine old and new on a day trip from Bratislava, taking in historic Devín Castle and nearby Devínska Kobyla Observation Tower

when to go

Hikers arrive from May to October, and the best conditions are at either end of the season. Come in spring for bluebells and purple delphiniums, or in September and October for cooler temperatures and autumn colours. December is the start of ski season in the High Tatras, while Christmas markets add sparkle to Bratislava and Košice.

how to get there

With tourism set to rise, it's no wonder budget airline carriers like Ryanair and Wizz Air have launched direct routes between the UK and Poprad, Slovakia's gateway to the Tatras. By rail, the daily Nightjet sleeper travels between Brussels and Vienna, which is less than an hour by train from Bratislava.

10
Armenia

GEORGIA

Haghpat and Sanahin Monasteries

Gyumri   Vanadzor

Haghartsin Monastery

AZERBAIJAN

Armenian Genocide Museum
Lavash and Lahmajun Gaidz

Yerevan   **Geghard Monastery**
Garni Temple

TURKEY

Noravank

AZER.

IRAN

highlights

1 / Visit **UNESCO-recognised monasteries** Geghard, Haghpat and Sanahin, as well as sun-kissed Noravank and 2000-year-old **Garni Temple**.

2 / Feast on **traditional dishes** like *tolma* (beef-stuffed vine leaves), *ghapama* (stuffed pumpkin), *lavash* (flatbread) and *khorovats* (grilled meat) at Lavash in Yerevan and try Western Armenian pizza at Lahmajun Gaidz.

3 / Experience the **Armenian Genocide Museum** in Yerevan – 2025 is the 110th anniversary of the start of the genocide.

4 / Stroll through wildflowers in springtime and visit the finely-restored **Haghartsin Monastery** on hikes around Dilijan.

A s the world's oldest Christian nation and a civilisation that dates back thousands of years, Armenia has plenty to look back on – but its future has plenty of potential too. Traditionally, travel to this South Caucasus nation focused on its magnificent monasteries, but now there's so much more. The country has marvellous hiking, including the brand new Armenia National Trail, and its wine scene is worth clinking a glass of Areni Noir to. Countries like Albania and Georgia got all the attention a few years ago; now it's Armenia's turn.

HIT THE TRAILS

Armenia's sparsely-populated mountains and valleys make for perfect hiking territory. Plus there are plenty of cute villages along the way happy to stuff you with *khorovats* (grilled meat) and give you a place to set up camp. Unveiled in 2024, the freshly-mapped 1000km (620 miles) Armenian

National Trail crosses the country length-wise and follows similar paths to the Transcaucasian Trail – an ongoing project meant to link Armenia with Georgia and Azerbaijan. Use the HikeArmenia app to find sections of either trail, as well as shorter, no less breathtaking routes that cross monastery-topped peaks. Or rent a car and go off the beaten track on a road trip. If you drive south from capital Yerevan, you'll find Silk Road merchant trails with *caravan-serai* (inns), and rarely visited territory over the Meghri Pass to the Iranian border. Or head up to the towns lining the gargantuan Debed Canyon, where lovely guesthouse matriarchs teach you how to bake *gata* (sweet paste-filled cake). Soviet-era *marshrutka* (shared taxis) are also an option for exploring if you want someone else to drive, though vehicles only leave when full.

MORE THAN MONASTERIES

A few hundred years after Jesus' death, a Christian named Gregory the Illuminator healed Armenian king Tiridates III, prompting the ruler to convert his whole kingdom to the religion – making it the first Christian nation in the world. The result is that these days Armenia is dotted with thousands of marvellous monasteries that are governed by the Armenian Catholic Apostolic Church. While these should be on any visitor's must-see list, plenty more awaits. Fly over a gorge via the world's longest cable car, Wings of

The magnificent four-peaked volcano of Mt Aragats, Armenia's highest point **1** Yerevan cityscape **2** Reliquary in Vagharshapat's Mother See of Holy Etchmiadzin, said to contain a fragment of Noah's Ark

Living in Armenia is a joy thanks to its vibrant culture and breathtaking land-scapes. When visiting, eat delicious *tolma*, explore ancient monasteries and enjoy Yerevan's fun and safe nightlife.

SIMELA NAMAVAR
/ Jazz singer

Tatev; gawk at freshly-refurbished tufa-stone architecture in Gyumri and Goris; ski in winter at the new Myler Mountain Resort; and float above Yerevan's Republic Square during the International Balloon Festival. If you love decaying Soviet architecture, Armenia has that in spades too – don't miss the telescopes around Byurakan and aban-doned warehouses in Alaverdi.

NEXT WINE DESTINATION

In its USSR days, Armenia was responsible for brewing brandy – very good brandy that famously had Winston Churchill addicted. But Armenian grapes tell a longer history. In 2007, archaeologists found wine making pottery more than 6000 years old – making the country the proud owner of the world's oldest winery. Since then, the buzz about Armenian wine and ancient grape varieties has inspired dozens of new producers, who are doing truly delicious things with both modern and natural techniques. And don't just take our word for it. Armenian wine frequently wins awards and the country

5

hosted the 2024 UNWTO Global Conference on Wine Tourism. The place to sample the local product is unquestionably the Areni region – Momik WineCube, Trinity Canyon and Old Bridge are all terrific vineyards, and there's an Areni Wine Festival in October too. Or visit the bars on Yerevan's Saryan St and enjoy Yerevan Wine Days in June. North, near Dilijan, Ijevan Wine Factory hosts engaging tours, and just completed construction on the country's largest tasting room as well as a traditional mill producing flour for favourite local flatbread, *lavash*.

3 Inside the UNESCO World Heritage-listed Sanahin Monastery **4** Cutting a slice of traditional Armenian *gata*, a delicious bread/cake hybrid **5** Khor Virap Monastery, just south of Yerevan at the foot of Mt Ararat

when to go

Early summer is prime time to visit thanks to pleasant temperatures and the Vardavar water festival. A winter visit isn't bad either, thanks to Yerevan's cultural venues, skiing and Jermuk's spas.

how to get there

Most flights go through capital Yerevan. Road border crossings are open with Iran and Georgia only. From the latter, take the train from Tbilisi or Batumi for a historic, slow journey.

further reading

Watch films by psychedelic filmmaker Sergei Parajanov and Armenian–Canadian Atom Egoyan; listen to Armenian–French tenor Charles Aznavour; and read *Operation Nemesis: The Assassination Plot that Avenged the Armenian Genocide* by Eric Bogosian.

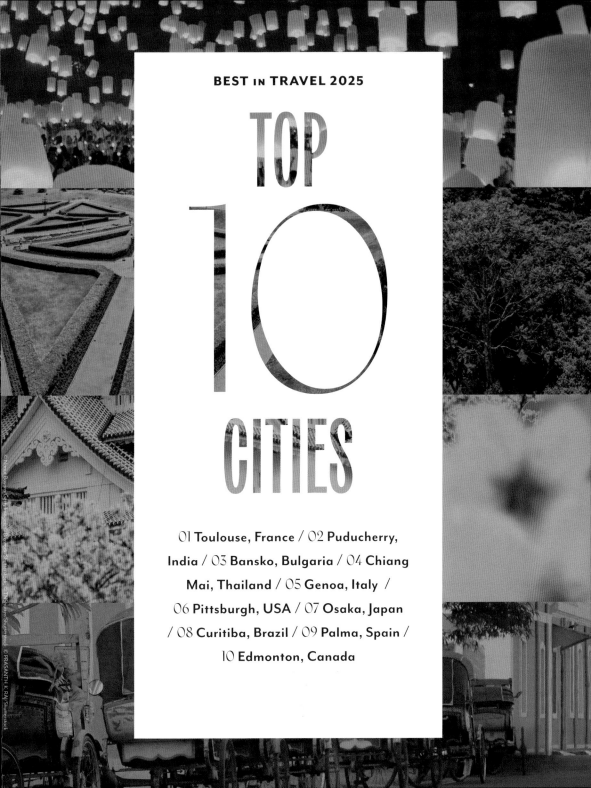

BEST in TRAVEL 2025

TOP 10 CITIES

01 Toulouse, France / 02 Puducherry, India / 03 Bansko, Bulgaria / 04 Chiang Mai, Thailand / 05 Genoa, Italy / 06 Pittsburgh, USA / 07 Osaka, Japan / 08 Curitiba, Brazil / 09 Palma, Spain / 10 Edmonton, Canada

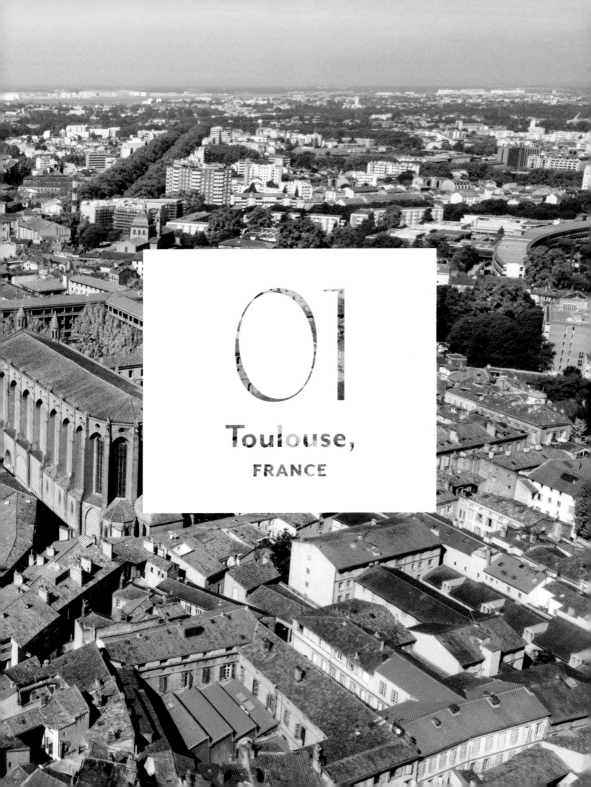

01

Toulouse,
FRANCE

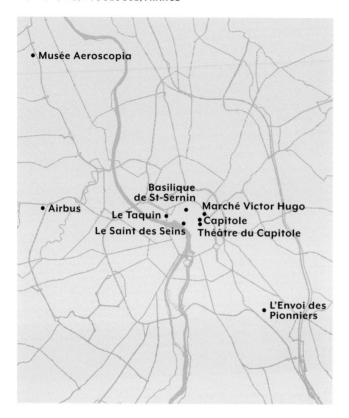

- Musée Aeroscopia
- Airbus
- Basilique de St-Sernin
- Le Taquin
- Le Saint des Seins
- Marché Victor Hugo
- Capitole
- Théâtre du Capitole
- L'Envoi des Pionniers

highlights

1 / Catch a live gig at **Le Saint des Seins**, jazz at **Le Taquin** or classical music at **Théâtre du Capitole** – Toulouse is a UNESCO City of Music after all.

2 / Take an architectural tour and don't miss Romanesque **Basilique St-Sernin** and neoclassical landmark **Capitole**.

3 / Deep-dive into Toulouse's unmatched aviation heritage at **Musée Aeroscopia**, **L'Envol des Pionniers** and **Airbus**.

4 / Shop for a picnic of local produce at **Marché Victor Hugo** or grab a cassoulet lunch in an eatery above the covered market.

P rovocative art galleries in upcycled industrial venues, a vibrant cafe life, top-drawer cuisine and restorative French *flânerie* along sun-spangled river and canal banks render this 'Paris in miniature' an appealing weekend-break destination. Toulouse is booming (its population is predicted to grow by 90,000 in the next decade) meaning now is the time to enjoy its captivating *art de vivre*.

NEW CULTURAL PICKINGS

Be it flying to the moon in a simulator mimicking the physical sensations an astronaut experiences at the Cité de l'Espace space museum, or seeking out backstreet workshops where artisans have revived the medieval craft of woad-dyeing to create

every shade of brilliant blue, Toulouse's cultural pickings surprise and delight.

In autumn 2025, the Musée des Augustins reopens after years of renovation. Inside a 14th-century convent complex, with cloister and rousing echoes of yesteryear monastic life filling its galleries, the museum has been Toulouse's art bastion since 1795. Stimulating new museography will finally make its world-class collection of 13th- to early 20th-century paintings and sculptures equally accessible to visitors with disabilities, and innovative trails through the displays will cast millennial perspectives on age-old masterpieces, encouraging visitors to explore more thoughtfully.

This follows the 2024 reopening of Fondation Bemberg, in a Renaissance *hôtel particulier* (mansion) built in 1562 for merchant Pierre II d'Assézat, who made his fortune in Toulouse trading woad. The treasure chest of Cranach to Post-Impressionist paintings, ceramics, majolica, enamels, marquetry and other *objets d'art* is dazzling. Other 'old-timer' art venues – Les Abattoirs Musée – Frac Occitanie Toulouse; Galerie Le Château d'Eau; Espaces EDF Bazacle – remain as edgy as the day they opened in a revamped abattoir, decommissioned water tower, mill-turned-hydroelectric power station, you name it.

CONTEMPORARY EPICUREAN

No visit to France is complete without a delicious dose of traditional French cuisine. Toulouse plays ball with bistros cooking up steaming bowls of *cassoulet* (duck, sausage and white-bean stew), markets overflowing with seasonal produce from the sun-soaked southwest and a holy trinity of duck,

Couvent des Jacobins and the coral-coloured Toulouse cityscape **1** The 200-year-old Jardin des Plantes offers a gentle respite from the buzz of central Toulouse **2** Choir stalls and altar of Romanesque Basilique St-Sernin

> The 9m-tall (29.5ft) mechanical Minotaur is an emblematic figure who resonates with the image of Toulouse, a labyrinthine city with incredible cultural projects, heritage and excellent food.

FRANÇOIS DELAROZIÈRE
/ Artistic director, Halle de la Machine

saucisse de Toulouse (local pork sausage) and Armagnac brandy in the kitchen. Chefs innovate at Les Halles de la Cartoucherie, a 2023 vintage in a repurposed munitions factory that is now a covered food hall, co-working space and concert venue in one.

PLAY THE FRENCH *FLANEUR*

While Toulouse locals look forward to the opening of a third metro line in 2025, for weekend visitors, old-school French *flânerie* (idle wandering) remains the finest means of getting around. This old Roman stronghold was rebuilt in pinkish terracotta brick – hence its nickname La Ville Rose (the Pink City) in the 17th century, and the best way to get under its skin is by walking the tree-shaded banks of the Garonne River and UNESCO-listed Canal du Midi, a waterway slicing through Toulouse on its 360km (200 miles) route across France from the Med to the Atlantic. Lose yourself in the car-free tangle of streets in the Vieux Quartier (Old Town) and among the student-fuelled cafe crowd on Place du

3 © SolStock/Getty Images 4 © Tupungato/Shutterstock 5 © BestPhotoStudio/Shutterstock

5

Capitole. Catch a whimsical menagerie of giant mechanical creatures out for a stroll from their HQ at Halle de la Machine – the wonderful urban street opera its theatre company staged in late 2024 will hopefully be repeated. Whatever you do, meander slowly to bathe in an iridescent kaleidoscope of reds, pinks and ambers spangled by the light of the sun and the moon, and feel the beat of this compelling, occasionally quirky, largely unsung city in France's hot south.

3 Alfresco food and wine in a Toulouse chateau 4 City life in the Capitole district 5 The Musée de l'Histoire de la Médecine on the banks of the Garonne River

when to go

Spring sees cafe tables spill across squares and markets burst with strawberries, asparagus and artichokes. Cruise by boat or bike along the canal and kayak or canoe on the river from June to September. Summer is festival season.

how to get there

Flights from dozens of European destinations land at Toulouse-Blagnac Airport, 7km (4.5 miles) northwest of the centre and linked by shuttle bus or taxi.

further reading

Antoine de Saint-Exupéry, early Toulouse aviator, philosopher and celebrity author of *The Little Prince*, evokes the thrill, danger and solitary nature of flying in his novel *Wine, Sand and Stars*.

02

Puducherry,
INDIA

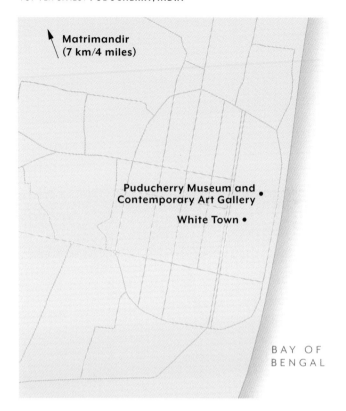

Matrimandir
(7 km/4 miles)

Puducherry Museum and
Contemporary Art Gallery

White Town

BAY OF
BENGAL

highlights

1 / Take a stroll through historic **White Town**, with its pastel-hued buildings that could just as easily be on the French Riviera.

2 / Check out the ever-changing displays at the government-run **Puducherry Contemporary Art Gallery**, which opened in 2022.

3 / See artefacts from the Chola and Vijayanagar empires displayed alongside elegant French antiques at the **Puducherry Museum**.

4 / Head north to Auroville to see the gilded **Matrimandir**, a non-religious temple where Aurovillians go not to meditate, but to concentrate.

O verlooking the Bay of Bengal in South India, Puducherry (formerly Pondicherry) has long enticed visitors with its Gallic architecture – a remnant of the city's status as an on-again, off-again French colony until 1954 – and its temples, churches and spiritual centres. It's also the closest city to Auroville, a spiritual-but-not-religious experimental township with residents hailing from around the world. Now, thanks to an extensive project designed to reclaim sandy beaches that eroded into the sea, Puducherry is reimagining itself as a top destination for lovers of sand and surf, too.

A SEASIDE RECLAIMED

While Puducherry has all the trappings of a coastal getaway, for the last three decades, it's been missing one key element: an actual beach. The sandy stretches of coastline that once flanked the city disappeared into oblivion in the early 1990s, an unexpected side effect of the 1989 construction of the

Pondicherry Harbour. Up until recently, visitors to Puducherry would either have to head out of town if they wanted to spend a day at the beach or simply stick to strolls along the city's 1.2km (0.7 miles) Promenade, separated from the Bay of Bengal by a stone seawall that came to be known as Rock Beach. Thanks to joint efforts by the local government and India's Central Marine Fisheries Research Institute, the city's sandy coastline is now being restored, largely with the use of artificial reefs designed to reshape the shore and attract fish to the area, a boon for local fishers. While strolling along the Rock Beach Promenade, cotton candy in hand, is still a popular way to soak up the city's vibes – particularly as the sun begins to set – patches of sandy beaches, including the aptly named New Beach, have begun to emerge. A massive reef installation project in 2023–24 hoped to bring back even more sand, helping Puducherry regain its former beachy glory.

SEEKING SPIRITUALITY

Although most of Puducherry's residents are Hindu, there's a large Catholic population, and the city's towering churches and cathedrals add to its architectural splendour. The most famous is the 18th-century Immaculate Conception Cathedral, a towering white edifice ornately adorned with yolk-yellow accents and sculptures

Gallic charm in Puducherry's French Quarter **1** A splash of colour along the city streets **2** The Jesuits' splendid Our Lady of the Immaculate Conception Cathedral

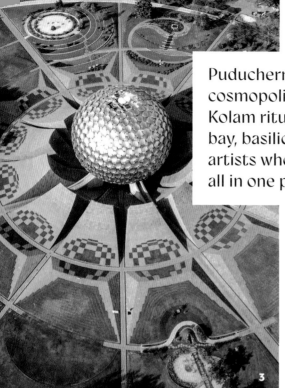

> Puducherry is rooted in its heritage yet cosmopolitan, with thousand-year-old Kolam rituals, games of *pétanque* by the bay, basilica bells and experimental sonic artists who invent their own instruments, all in one place.

SID SAIKIA
/ Innkeeper, Gratitude Heritage

of angels. Equally eye-catching, Our Lady of the Angels is characterised by a light coral-hued Greco-Roman facade with twin columns flanking its entry. Inside, Corinthian pilasters support a massive arched ceiling.

Yet despite Puducherry's abundance of churches, it is still very much a Hindu city. In fact, you can't walk far before stumbling upon – and possibly into – a Dravidian temple crowned with a conical *vimana* (tower) and bedecked with brightly hued sculptures of ethereal entities and animals. Among the most popular is centuries-old Manakula Vinayagar Temple in the White Town neighbourhood. It's dedicated to Ganesh, the elephant-headed remover of obstacles in the Hindu pantheon, and houses numerous colourful friezes depicting mythological scenes.

Another big draw is the Sri Aurobindo Ashram, established by politician-turned-yogi Sri Aurobindo and his French collaborator, Mirra Alfassa, better known as 'The Mother'. Aspirants come here to practice the ashram's signature Integral Yoga, while curious sightseers can take a three-hour tour of the ashram and the numerous craft

3 © Vyas Abhishek/Shutterstock 4 © Dinodia Photo/Getty Images 5 © Sultan Frederic/Getty Images

5

workshops that support it. The Mother's efforts didn't stop with the ashram – she was also the driving force behind the establishment of Auroville, an intentional community just north of town. Founded in 1968 as a 'universal town where men and women of all countries are able to live in peace and progressive harmony above all creeds, all politics and all nationalities', Auroville continues to draw in visitors from across the planet. Many come to see the community's centrepiece Matrimandir, a golden golf-ball-esque geodesic dome housing a giant glass sphere.

3 Matrimandir at Sri Aurobindo Ashram **4** Puja offerings prepared for Puducherry's Masi Magam festival **5** Dusk over the city and the Notre Dame des Anges church

when to go

Puducherry has two monsoons: one from July to September and a second from October to December. Come between January and March for cool and dry weather.

how to get there

The city has a small airport with limited domestic service – most people fly into Chennai International Airport, 145km (90 miles) away, and then hire a taxi or take a bus the rest of the way.

further reading

Philosophical novel *Life of Pi* by Yann Martel is partially set in Puducherry. Akash Kapur's *Better to Have Gone: Love, Death, and the Quest for Utopia in Auroville* tells the story of early Auroville through the lens of some of its first residents.

03

Bansko,
BULGARIA

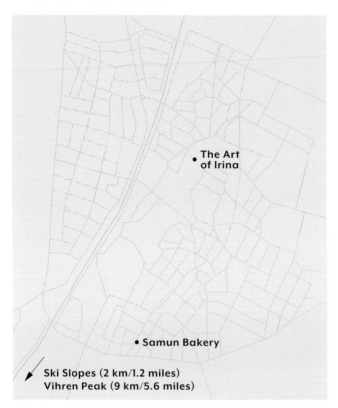

**The Art
of Irina**

• Samun Bakery

**Ski Slopes (2 km/1.2 miles)
Vihren Peak (9 km/5.6 miles)**

highlights

1 / Hike with locals up **Vihren peak** for the sunrise on 1 July as part of the July Morning celebration.

2 / Breakfast on a *banitsa* – a traditional morning pastry with cheese – at **Samun bakery**.

3 / Embrace winter in Bansko and **go skiing** on the slopes from December to April.

4 / Support a local gem at **The Art of Irina** – this Bansko artist is known for her satirical paintings that serve as a unique souvenir from your travels.

Bansko, a small town nestled among the majestic peaks of Bulgaria's Pirin Mountains, has been a favourite ski destination for decades. Over the last few years, however, a new trend has emerged and turned this quaint village into a popular hotspot for remote workers. It's now on the world map of the best digital nomad destinations, attracting adrenaline seekers and location-independent professionals from all backgrounds. Bansko is quickly shifting its image from just a winter resort to a desirable all-year-round holiday and work paradise.

CATCH THE WAVE

The magic of Bansko lies partly in its relaxed and new-found multicultural vibe. The tight-knit and welcoming community of expats, international nomads and Bulgarian locals helps recent arrivals meet like-minded people from day one. It's easier to form meaningful connections more quickly here than in any big town around the world.

Thanks to the international influence, many new places have been popping up in the past years – craft beer shops, cosy cafes, modern bakeries. Add the low living costs, exceptional climate, natural surroundings and rich social life and Bansko is becoming a top alternative to other better-known travel destinations.

Despite the cosmopolitan atmosphere and recent fame, you can still experience traditional Bulgarian celebrations here. January is the month to see the famous Kukeri, marching through town with their elaborate costumes. On 14 February, locals celebrate Wine Day instead of Valentine's, with many wineries in the area opening their doors to visitors. In the month of March, you'll see red-white bracelets on sale every-where in town, said to bring health and good luck. And during the Easter holidays in May, locals paint and 'fight' with boiled eggs.

Traditions are also preserved in the local cuisine. When you visit a local *mehana* (tavern) you'll be served age-old recipes with locally sourced ingredients in an authentic setting. The region's most celebrated dishes include *kapama* (sour cabbage and meat), *banski starets* (sausage), *chomlek* (veal and potatoes) and more.

SMALL TOWN, BIG FUN

Don't be fooled by the size of Bansko – it might be a small town but it has plenty of activities and events of all sizes happen-ing year-round. From mountain biking,

A bird's-eye view of Bansko **1** Vihren peak, in the Pirin Mountains above town **2** Pay a visit to a traditional Bansko *mehana* (tavern) to sample local speciality dishes

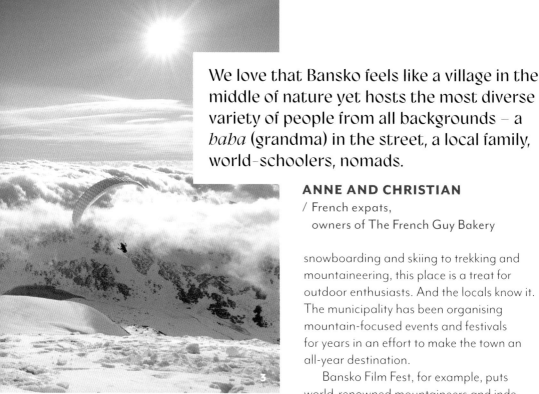

We love that Bansko feels like a village in the middle of nature yet hosts the most diverse variety of people from all backgrounds – a *baba* (grandma) in the street, a local family, world-schoolers, nomads.

ANNE AND CHRISTIAN
/ French expats,
   owners of The French Guy Bakery

snowboarding and skiing to trekking and mountaineering, this place is a treat for outdoor enthusiasts. And the locals know it. The municipality has been organising mountain-focused events and festivals for years in an effort to make the town an all-year destination.

Bansko Film Fest, for example, puts world-renowned mountaineers and independent adventure filmmakers on the same stage to showcase their work. There's also the Bansko Jazz Festival, an open-air event attracting musicians and jazz fans from around the world. An open-air Opera Festival, Rock Festival and many other cultural activities fill the rest of Bansko's events calendar in other months.

The rise of digital nomadism in town led to the creation of a very particular new festival – Bansko Nomad Fest. This brings hundreds of freelancers, remote-work professionals and entrepreneurs together to celebrate the location-independent lifestyle and share their experiences. It's one of the biggest such events in the world, with a week-long agenda of insightful workshops, inspiring lectures, networking events, adventure trips and more.

3 © Maya Karkalicheva Getty Images 4 © MstudioG Shutterstock 5 © Maya Karkalicheva Getty Images

5

LOCAL CHARM

Bansko has a decades-long history of welcoming foreigners, but its true appeal lies in the locals. Breaking through their initial reserve unveils the true essence of Bulgarian hospitality. And remember, Bansko is only one of the many wonders of the wider Balkan region. Consider the town the first chapter of your journey, an invitation to discover much more beauty lying beyond its abundant charms.

3 Paragliding in the Pirin Mountains **4** Quiet charm and perfect peaks in central Bansko **5** From hiking and mountain biking to winter snowsports, the dramatic countryside around Bansko promises endless outdoor adventure

when to go

Enjoy Bansko's winter sports in March and April when it's quieter. June to September promises open-air events, festivals, cultural activities and outdoor adventures.

how to get there

Bansko is easily accessible, with a direct bus from Sofia Airport or public buses from the capital's central bus station. Renting a car from the airport is also easy; it's a two-hour drive to Bansko.

04

Chiang Mai,
THAILAND

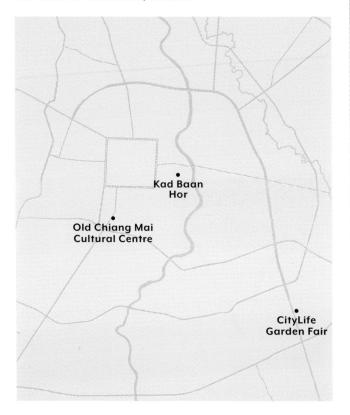

Kad Baan Hor

Old Chiang Mai Cultural Centre

CityLife Garden Fair

highlights

1 / Experience **Chiang Mai Food Festival**, a yearly event held in January celebrating the best food the city has to offer.

2 / Support the long-standing, fundraising **Citylife Garden Fair**, best known for its boozy food markets and auctioned giveaways.

3 / Wander Friday morning's **Kad Baan Hor Market** where Yunnanese Muslims and tribespeople sell food unlike anything else in the city.

4 / Belly up to the all-you-can eat *khantoke* dinner, accompanied by traditional theatre performances, at Old Chiang Mai Cultural Centre.

From simple greetings that skip 'hello' and dive in with a 'have you eaten yet?' to heated national debates on what type of vegetable is an acceptable addition to a holy basil stir-fry, there are more dimensions to Thai cuisine than sweet, sour, salt and spice. And Chiang Mai takes the country's love affair with unique flavours to new heights. While you can join pre-planned food tours, crafting your own journey from back-market stall to thousand-dollar gastronomic journey can prove to be far more rewarding, and a lot tastier to boot.

START AT THE MARKET

The best way to experience real Thai cuisine is at its source – the market. While raw ingredients take precedent, there's a few spots to check out on your first foray into

Thai food that'll set you off on the right track. Kad Luang, otherwise known as Warorot, is Chiang Mai's oldest and largest market, a place of trade since the foundation of the city back in 1296. The bottom floor of the main hall is dedicated to food, with Northern Thai staples such as spicy *sai oua* sausage, pork rinds and young-chilli dip in abundance. Dam Rong is the locals' preferred vendor for such delicacies, while the sweet coconut and pandan flavours of Thai Sweets Under the Stairs can help cut through the spice.

SAMPLE NORTHERN THAI SPECIALITIES

As your tour delves deeper into the city, the unique and robust Northern Thai cuisine should take centre stage. Han Thueng Chiang Mai restaurant is a local favourite that serves up authentic Northern dishes that are as bold as they are fiery. If you're adventurous, try their Bib Gourmand–recommended ant-egg omelettes and jungle-sourced specials. Alternatively, Tong Tem Toh on Nimmanhaemin Rd offers a platter of Northern hors d'oeuvres that are perfect for the uninitiated, while Huan Soontaree, set along the tranquil River Ping, provides an unforgettable dining experience with nightly performances by the famous Lanna folk singer, Soontaree Vechanont.

The city's lovechild, *khao soi*, is probably its most famous dish. This rich coconut curry noodle soup originated in Chiang Mai and recently shot to fame when it was selected as the world's best soup by *TasteAtlas*. For the original, head to well-known Khao Soi Lung Prakit Kad Kom;

Dragon staircase of Wat Phra That Doi Suthep
1 Street-food stalls in Chiang Mai **2** Dig in to the city's alluring Northern Thai specialities

Northern Laap spicy meat salad incorporates cumin, blood and bile. It's recently gone from dying dish to number one choice for hungry teens. Try Laap Bunker or Laap Duang Dee Mee Suk for an authentic taste.

GOVIT THATARAT
/ Founder, *Review Chiang Mai*

3 © enviromantic/Getty Images

or if you're feeling bold, head to Khao Soi Nimman, where the large menu of alternative toppings will test your taste buds.

Chiang Mai is also a perfect place to sample authentic Shan and Burmese cuisine. The Swan Burmese Cuisine may be the city's most popular restaurant for the latter, but Free Bird Cafe's light bites come with a helping of social development that's worth supporting, while Payod Shan Food is where you can find truly authentic tribal food that also happens to be vegan.

CULINARY HEAD-TURNERS

Michelin-recommended spots litter the map too. Blackitch Artisan Kitchen, with its sustainably sourced 10-course meal featuring a fusion of Thai, Japanese and Chinese influences, is a culinary journey that defies expectations. Loin.cnx has high-concept Thai flavours and artistic presentation. And the celebrity status of chef Nan's tasting menus at Cuisine de Garden showcase the real creativity of an old-time Chiang Mai foodie.

TOP FIVE
Unusually Delicious Dining Spots in Chiang Mai

1 / **Blackitch Artisan Kitchen:** Locally sourced tasting menus that journey through the most abstract ingredients.

2 / **Mont Nom Sod:** Established in 1964, 'Milk and Toast' is the real OG when it comes to sweet toppings on toast.

3 / **Laap Bunker:** Best known for serving raw-meat salads and barbecued innards, tapas-style.

4 / **Beef Satay Under Ton Khoi:** Sit on tiny wooden stools roadside and enjoy beef satay with an unusual peanut dip.

5 / **Gob Oua Sansai:** Spicy sausage-meat-stuffed frog, grilled to perfection.

For a final twist to your self-made gastronomic outing, dig into hearty American food at Dinky's BBQ or sample authentic East Asian fare at one of over a hundred Japanese restaurants. Whether you're a seasoned gourmet or just a curious traveller, Chiang Mai's culinary landscape offers something new and exciting at every turn. It's time to book your ticket to this gastronomic paradise.

3 Lunch is served in Chiang Mai **4** The city's Wat Lok Moli temple complex, dressed to impress for November's Loi Krathong (Lantern Festival) **5** Monks release *khom loy* (lanterns) during Loi Krathong at the Old City's Wat Phan Tao

how to get there

Chiang Mai is located in the north of Thailand, just an hour's flight from the capital of Bangkok. Those on a budget can opt for a bus or train ride, both clocking in about 8-10 hours respectively. Most of the city's best food can be found near the Old City and Nimmanhaemin Rd, while out-of-town spots can be hit or miss. But why stop at tasting? Thai Farm Cooking School invites you to learn the art of Northern Thai cooking first-hand, while Thai Akha Cooking School uses ingredients and teaches techniques straight from the jungle.

05

Genoa,
ITALY

Old Port

**Pasticceria
Marescotti di Cavo**

• **Palazzi dei Rolli**

• **Mercato Orientale**

LIGURIAN SEA

Boccadasse
•

Like all great port cities, Genoa is a world unto itself. Ebbing and flowing along the northern spine of the Italian peninsula, the Ligurian capital city's potent vibrancy is enclosed by the jagged, almost forbidding coastline that surrounds it. Those who know Genoa jealously guard it, fearing that its power might become diluted by becoming too well known. But a city capable of raising a mighty fleet, amassing untold riches and turning basil into pesto deserves every accolade. It also deserves to be on your list of the next best places to discover.

THE SMART CITY BREAK

At a time when we are looking to travel with sustainability in mind, Genoa stands as a unique example of just how much can be done when you're willing to get creative in bringing the ancient and modern together.

highlights

1 / Wander through the alleyways known locally as *caruggi* to capture the soul of the city and discover the sumptuous **Palazzi dei Rolli**.

2 / Indulge in endless versions of **pesto** (ideally on *trofie* pasta or focaccia) at the **Mercato Orientale**—and everywhere else.

3 / Have your mind blown at the **aquarium** and **biosphere** at Genoa's Old Port.

4 / Get your morning (or afternoon) coffee at **Pasticceria Marescotti di Cavo** on Via di Fossatello.

5 / Walk the coastline to tiny **Boccadasse** and experience Cinque Terre vibes without leaving the city.

The city has long been a familiar destination to travellers by sea – its port is the second-largest in Italy and one of the largest in the Mediterranean. But when travel was restricted during the pandemic, domestic visitors became the main source of tourism revenue, leading residents and businesses to think differently about what they might offer. This led to the Tourism Friendly Cities project, an EU-sponsored dialogue between visitors, residents and businesses to create accessible, resilient communities in medium-sized cities.

This renaissance has brought initiatives like Levante Waterfront, a near-net-zero residential and commercial development headed by famed architect and native Genovese Renzo Piano. Digitisation has also moved quickly: the Genoa City Pass grants access to all of the city's museums and attractions via an app that visitors can download for free on their mobile phones, and the BlueMed project means that digital nomads can count on high-speed internet. Couple this with the urban renewal programmes and an already iconic aquarium, and you've got the perfect escape.

A SEDUCTIVE CITY CENTRE

Genoa's history and topography have formed a unique urban environment where snaking alleys known as *caruggi* often link up with hidden treasures full of the sort of wealth and decadence you'd expect to find in Florence or Rome. Thanks to private

Colourful houses in Boccadasse, a Genoa neighbourhood that was once an old fishing village **1** Via Garibaldi in Genoa's atmospheric Old City **2** Gothic–Romanesque opulence inside Genoa's zebra-striped Cattedrale di San Lorenzo

There's something special about Genoa. Like many families, we moved abroad to find new opportunities, before, like many families, we realised that everything we needed was waiting for us at home.

CAROLINA
/ Local pastry chef

reinvestment, noble residences that once housed visiting dignitaries – such as the UNESCO-listed Palazzi dei Rolli – are being transformed into boutique hotels, chic gallery spaces and immersive museums. Wandering through the dense labyrinth of the ancient centre is an almost heady experience – it's easy to become intoxicated by the smells and sounds that vibrate off the thick stone walls. This is a city embraced by time, not trapped in it.

Speaking of smells, Genoa is a destination not just for food lovers, but for food scholars. Time your visit for early spring and snag a ticket to the Pesto World Championship. If you can't make it to the competition, you can always head to the Mercato Orientale, the historic food market in the heart (or the belly) of the city. Feast on focaccia and revel in ravioli as locals chat in Ligurian dialects.

JUST CONNECTED ENOUGH

Genoa's mountainous terrain has historically meant that getting there from the rest of Italy involved long car rides or even longer train journeys. But with the completion of the new, high-speed Terzo Valico railway scheduled for 2026 (with some possibly operational beforehand), the city will be easily reachable from

Turin and Piedmont. There's also a municipal plan to have the entire city connected by electric transport by mid-2025, along with 70km (43.5 miles) of cycling lanes.

Although high-speed rail links from Rome and Milan are still some way off, Genoa is becoming more accessible for short visits, and with the ever-increasing popularity of the Cinque Terre and Portofino, the city is a great place to be based for a longer look around Liguria.

3 Feast on freshly baked, olive-oil-drenched foccacia, a Genovese speciality **4** Cheese, charcuterie and deli delights in the Mercato Orientale **5** Courtyard at Palazzo Doria-Tursi, part of the Musei di Strada Nuova **6** Sunset over Manarola in the Cinque Terre, an easy side-trip from Genoa

when to go

Genoa sparkles from spring to autumn, with sultry summers in the middle. If you're planning to explore the Ligurian coast by boat from the city, don't be surprised if squalls hinder your plans in March, April and October.

how to get there

Regional trains run from Rome (5½ hours) and Milan (2 hours) throughout the day and cost less than €20. The Genoa City Airport has services to and from several European cities.

06
Pittsburgh,
USA

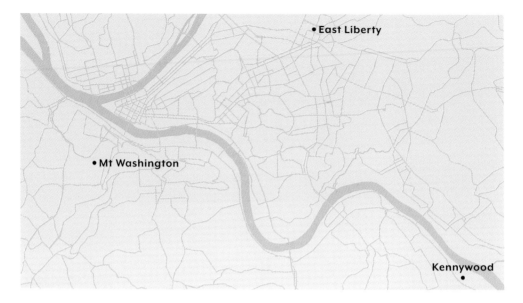

The most recent renaissance of Pittsburgh, a city firmly rooted in its geographic perch at the intersection of three rivers and generations-old immigrant traditions, is a pitch perfect dynamism marked by old favourites and new gems, often side by side: ethnic enclaves, odes to cultural icons like Andy Warhol and Roberto Clemente abound, and a trend-setting modernity fuelling the food and drink scene. The city's affordability makes it attractive, low-key and unpretentious. Its flavours and cultural heritage are authentic and genuine. Its appetite for growth and reinvention – fired first by steel, manufacturing and the industrial revolution, more recently by tech, education and healthcare – ambitious and often visionary. Pittsburgh is an ideal as much as a destination.

highlights

1 / Pull up to a communal table in the beer hall of bright, cheerful Lorelei for an incredible cocktail or wood-fired pizza in **East Liberty**, another neighbourhood redefining itself.

2 / Have fun at **Kennywood**, an iconic amusement park just 20 minutes from downtown whose storied past landed it on the National Historic Landmark register. Its century-old wooden roller coasters – yes, plural – are a must.

3 / Ride the **Duquesne Incline** from Station Square up to Mt Washington for stunning perspectives of the city and the three rivers. Restaurants at the top offer incredible views and menus.

LAWRENCEVILLE, PA

These days, you can't really talk about a trip to Pittsburgh without spending time in Lawrenceville. A ten-minute drive northeast of downtown along the southern riverfront of the Allegheny River, Lawrenceville's decade-long rise to 'it' neighbourhood has reimagined the Butler Street corridor – divided into Upper, Central and Lower Lawrenceville – as a walkable series of coffee shops, boutique stores and independently-owned restaurants and breweries that cover all budgets, from high-end to hole-in-the-wall.

Lawrenceville's location on the Allegheny made it first a valuable arsenal hub during the American Civil War before its industrial period in iron and steel through the 1900s. In the second half of the 20th century, like many other Western Pennsylvania communities, it fell victim to the economic depression that ravaged the area with the collapse of the steel industry.

Lawrenceville's modern moment, complete with notes of hipster grit and a sheen of approachable sophistication, is not immune to a familiar debate: is its success story one of reinvention or gentrification?

No matter where you land in that debate, the area's meteoric growth and loyal following are undeniable. And they bring plenty of foot traffic to the businesses that drive its cultural relevance: the local music venues like Spirit and Thunderbird Cafe, independent movie theatre Row House Cinema, art galleries and reservations-only Roberto

Pittsburgh at dusk from Mt Washington **1** Views over the city and the Monongahela and Allegheny Rivers from the Duquesne Incline **2** The eclectic frontage of Randyland art museum, in the Mexican War Streets historic district

© ESB Professional/Shutterstock **1** © ESB Professional/Shutterstock **2** © peeterv/Getty Images

> Pittsburgh's affordability makes it accessible – for small business owners, for artists, for tech start-ups, for restaurateurs – and it's accessibility makes it vibrant.

PETE KURZWEG
/ Owner of Lorelei, Independent Brewing and Hidden Harbor

Clemente Museum, celebrating Pittsburgh's entrenched sports legacy and honouring the life and legacy of the famed humanitarian, activist and Pittsburgh Pirates right fielder in a historic firehouse.

STROLLING THE STRIP

Starting just a block from downtown, Pittsburgh's Strip District, aka the 'Strip', is a friendly, down-to-earth, boisterous 1.2 sq km (0.5 sq miles) that's still the charming local favourite it's been for decades, an abundant mix of personalities and commerce that both hint at the city's hardscrabble roots and bring them to life for a new generation.

Starting at the Heinz History Museum, an ode to Pittsburgh's past, and walking northeast on Penn Avenue, the Strip is an easy place to while away a morning or afternoon with a coffee and fresh biscotti in hand. Italian and Asian markets neighbour each other, flanked by produce stands and sidewalk vendors selling everything from Steelers T-shirts to homemade Polish *pierogi* dumplings. You might pop into the original location of Primanti Brothers for Pittsburgh's iconic signature sandwich stuffed with vinegar-based coleslaw and French fries, or head to the nearby Terminal which houses a

3 © Egswoker/Getty Images 4 © PaulMcKinnon/Getty Images 5 © Althom/Getty Images

modern food hall inside a renovated warehouse. Even on a frosty winter weekend, the neighborhood's easy atmosphere bring buoyant crowds.

THREE IS THE MAGIC NUMBER

Pittsburgh's Three Sisters are a trio of identical bridges at Sixth, Seventh and Ninth Sts, named for local legends Roberto Clemente, Andy Warhol and Rachel Carson respectively. They connect downtown to the North Side over the Allegheny River and were commissioned in the late 1920s – their bright yellow suspension style is an iconic reference in any photograph of Pittsburgh's downtown.

3 Butler Street corridor in the revitalised Lawrenceville district
4 The Andy Warhol Museum, the city's ode to its most famous native son **5** Get a bird's-eye view of Pittsburgh's trio of rivers and city skyline from the top of Mt Washington

when to go

Pittsburgh's winters can be biting, especially along the riverfront, but perfect for a warm plate of homemade *pierogi*. Summers are lush – local greenergy abounds – but often thick with heat humidity, the kind that can best be cooled by a cold craft beer. Spring and autumn bring the most manageable and versatile temperatures, the latter with the benefit of stunning fall foliage.

how to get there

Pittsburgh's International Airport is an easy 20 minutes from downtown. It's also a great road trip destination: 5 to 6 hours from points along the East Coast and a great stop along the way when driving across the Midwest.

07

Osaka,
JAPAN

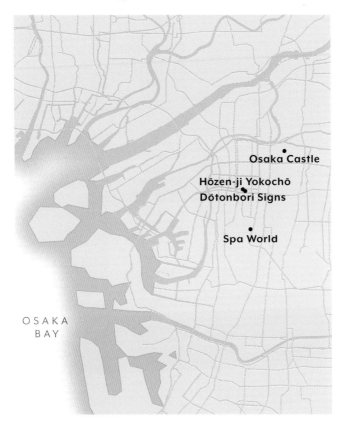

Osaka Castle

Hōzen-ji Yokochō
Dōtonbori Signs

Spa World

OSAKA
BAY

highlights

1 / Have your camera ready for **Dōtonbori's signs** – the warm glow of this district's neon lights will linger in your memory forever.

2 / Follow beautiful cobble-stone path **Hōzenji Yokochō** up to Hōzenji Temple, stop-ping at the tiny restaurants and cafes en route.

3 / Explore the majestic white fortress that is **Osaka Castle** – it's a 1930s recon-struction, but impressive nonetheless, with an excellent museum inside.

4 / Soak in **Spa World**, an *onsen* (Japanese bath house) amusement park where hot water and a little kitsch combine.

J apan's third-largest city shines, quite literally in its neon decked neighbourhoods, standing out in more ways than one. This former trading port is known for being a forward-thinking arts hub, nightlife centre with a thriv-ing LGBTIQ+ scene, gastronomy haven no matter your tastes and home to some of the best street-food vendors, live-music haunts and record shops in the country. Osaka always promises a lot of fun, but in 2025, the mighty Expo is back, giving the city a second chance at throwing the best World's Fair of all time.

EXPO RETURNS

It feels incredibly apt that Expo, the world's largest show of innovative design and scien-tific invention, is back in Osaka for a second time – the city is, after all, one of the most open-minded and dynamic in the country. It's the first city in Japan to hold the fair twice, 55 years apart, following their very successful turn hosting the cultural extravaganza in 1970 – which was the most highly attended Expo of the 20th century. You can still visit the extremely vibesy Tower of the Sun monument in the Expo Commemorative Park, before checking out the dazzling new site on Yumeshima Island in the former dockyards. With a title of 'Designing Future Society for Our Lives', the show, which will run from 13 April to 13 October 2025, promises to be thought-provoking, mind-expanding and, of course, socially conscious, inviting public interaction before, during and after the event at the People's Living Lab. Equally as exciting is the space itself – cutting-edge architects have designed the halls, pavilions and spaces, keeping the tradition of impressive Expo buildings in rude health.

EAT TILL YOU DROP

Osaka has a well-earned reputation as a food-lover's paradise and is the home of two of Japan's tastiest dishes: *okonomiyaki*, a pancake-like omelette of layered veggies, meat or seafood; and *takoyaki*, doughballs filled with minced or diced octopus, ginger and onion. What's unusual about the city's food scene when pitted against the rest of the country is that it's relatively easy to find vegan, vegetarian or halal versions of their famous dishes. Try OKO, who've just doubled their floor space and serve

Osaka Castle in the springtime *sakura* (cherry blossom) season **1** Neon lights up the night over Osaka Bay **2** The city's street-food stalls specialise in Osaka's signature *takoyaki*: gingery, octopus-filled doughballs

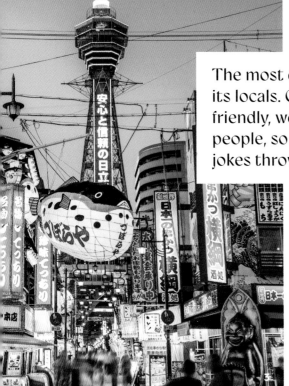

> The most distinct aspect about the city is its locals. Osakans are some of Japan's most friendly, welcoming and comedy-loving people, so conversations will always have jokes thrown in.

JONATHAN LUCAS
/ MICE Promotions specialist, Osaka

excellent vegan *okonomiyaki* and vegan and/or gluten free *takoyaki*; or Genji-soba for the best vegan, vegetarian and gluten free *soba* and ramen options in town. The city's gastro game has not gone unnoticed and Asia's first Time Out Food Market will be opening in the recently regenerated green space, Umekita Park, just a few hundred yards northwest of Osaka train station.

UPPING THE ART GAME

Osaka City Museum of Fine Arts, Osaka Museum of Natural History, Museum of Oriental Ceramics, Osaka Science Museum, Osaka Museum of History and Nakanoshima Museum of Art are all uniting in 2025 to bring one vast, co-curated exhibition, Osaka-Haku, to the public, a seamless display of artefacts that best represent the history and culture of the city. Each museum has selected 20 'Osaka Treasures', both ancient and modern, collected and handed down over generations, so this year visitors can really get to the heart of the city's richness and charm, through the history, arts, science and craft. Aside from these

3. © Nikada/Getty Images 4. © dvophotos/Shutterstock 5. © NU singer/Shutterstock 6. © Torsuza Thailand/Shutterstock

5

6

large institutions, small, new galleries are continuing to open across the city, giving independent visual artists opportunities to showcase their work. There's also a growing street-art scene and a push for mural artists to contribute to the cityscape, such as the Osaka-based collective WALL SHARE.

3 Tsūten-kaku observation tower, a retro symbol of the Shin-Sekai district **4** Take a dip in Osaka's traditional Japanese *onsen* **5** Blazing fall colours in Meiji no Mori Minō Park, just outside Osaka **6** Offerings to the Fudō Myō-ō statue at the tiny temple of Hōzen-ji

when to go

Late March through early May is cherry blossom (aka *sakura*) season and a super-popular time to visit. Halloween is extremely fun in Osaka.

how to get there

Osaka has two airports with direct flights landing from capital cities across Asia. If you're arriving in Tokyo, you can get to Osaka on the Shinkansen bullet train in 2½ hours.

08

Curitiba,

BRAZIL

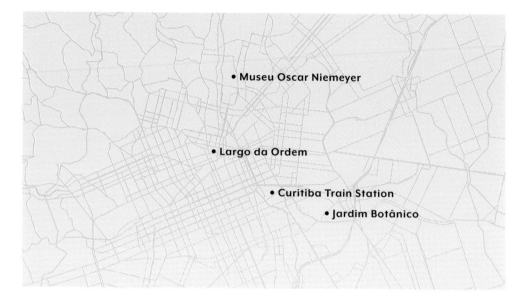

Museu Oscar Niemeyer

Largo da Ordem

Curitiba Train Station

Jardim Botânico

This famously progressive metropolis in Paraná state is a longtime leader in urban planning and sustainable development, and visiting might well leave you feeling a little more optimistic about climate mitigation. While Curitiba's green roots were planted in the 1970s, ongoing initiatives continue to inspire change. Recent innovations include a solar pyramid on a former landfill site, biodiverse honey gardens in urban parks and a bike-sharing scheme.

GETTING AROUND BY E-BUS & E-BIKE

As one of 20 founder members of the global C40 cities network (a worldwide alliance of 96 mayors dedicated to tackling climate change), Curitiba has long been at the forefront of urban planning and the city is regularly used as a test case for new environmental initiatives. Its integrated BRT (bus rapid transit) system, which utilises articulated vehicles and space-age tubular station pods throughout

highlights

1 / Appreciate art, sculpture and an exhibit about architect Niemeyer at **Museu Oscar Niemeyer**, a striking museum that still looks modern 20 years after it opened.

2 / Smell the flowers in the **Jardim Botânico**, a slice of greenery with sculpture, water features, paths and an elegant greenhouse.

3 / Wander **Largo da Ordem**, a cobblestone nexus in the heart of the city surrounded by historic edifices in a range of styles.

4 / Take a sublime train ride between Curitiba and Morretes through mountains and rainforest on the **Serra Verde Express**.

the metro area, has been copied in over 150 other cities. The BRT began introducing hybrid electric-biodiesel buses in the early 2010s and, in 2023, it road-tested South America's first two completely electric buses. With 70 additional vehicles now on order, you can expect to see an increasing number of e-buses in operation in 2025 as Curitiba works to make one-third of its fleet electric by 2030.

E-bikes are another game-changer. Curitiba introduced a city-wide bike-sharing program in 2023, ordering an initial stock of 500 bikes, half of them electric. The sleek two-wheeled machines can be unlocked by using a QR code and mobile app, and quickly recharged afterwards in modern smart stations. There are currently 250km (155 miles) of cycling lanes in and around the centre with plans to expand the network to 400km (249 miles) by 2025.

SUSTAINABLE PARKS

A visual highlight of Curitiba are its extensive parks, with 48 green spaces spread around the city. But look closely and you'll see there are also brains behind the beauty. One of the metropolis' largest parks, Barigui, powers its onsite facilities through a small hydroelectric plant using an artificial waterfall and lake, and more parks may soon follow suit.

Barigui and other urban areas are also helping to roll out a citywide honey garden programme which seeks to conserve native bee populations and subsequently stimulate

Parque Tanguá in northern Curitiba, just one of the city's 48 parks **1** The dramatic Museu Oscar Niemeyer building **2** The Serra Verde Express, making its greenery-swathed way through the mountains between Curitiba and Morretes

© gonthagon/Shutterstock **1** © Samuel Eriksen/Shutterstock **2** © cabaason/Shutterstock

> A city is only good for tourists if it's good for its citizens. Curitiba always innovates and takes care of maintenance. Tourists don't just visit tourist attractions, they experience our city.

TISA KASTRUP
/ Communication and curation,
  Curitiba Tourism

productivity in Curitiba's burgeoning urban farms. Flamboyant shrubs such as scarlet sage, hydrangeas and Japanese jasmine are planted to attract insects and are supplemented by other bushes and trees. Proactive city mayor, Rafael Greca, has pledged to plant 100,000 trees a year in Curitiba going forward. Walk through downtown's fecund squares and you'll quickly be engulfed in salubrious greenery – Praça Osorio at the west end of pedestrianised Calçadão da XV is like a mini slice of the Amazon, while Praça Santos Andrade to the east is a sanctuary of floral symmetry.

GREEN GOURMET

Alongside its honey gardens, Curitiba's support for urban farming programmes includes many highly productive community gardens, built on reclaimed degraded land and now forging intimate relationships with local restaurants. Manu, the city's most celebrated eating joint, won the Flor de Caña sustainable restaurant award in 2023 in recognition of its ethical food sourcing and

5

work with community groups. The restaurant cooperates closely with local fishers and stages workshops to educate people about food waste and the effective use of vegetables. Manu also maintains beehives on its property, and its chef-owner, Manoella Buffara, an alumnus of three-Michelin-star restaurant Noma in Copenhagen, was named Latin America's Best Female Chef in 2022 in the prestigious San Pellegrino and Acqua Panna awards.

3 Statuary in the Jardim Botânico glasshouse **4** Dragon fruit and sugar apples in the Mercado Municipal de Curitiba **5** Up-high views of Curitiba's city skyline and the expanse of the Jardim Botânico

when to go

Curitiba's subtropical climate is pleasant year-round. The winter months (June-August) are the coolest and driest.

how to get there

Afonso Pena International Airport has connections to most large Brazilian cities as well as Buenos Aires and Santiago de Chile. Curitiba's long-distance bus station is part of a single three-block complex called the *rodoferroviária*. Inter-city buses run by various private companies serve destinations from Rio de Janeiro to Buenos Aires.

further reading

Urban Acupuncture by Jaime Lerner, Curitiba's visionary ex-mayor, explores how to make cities more vibrant and liveable.

09

Palma,

SPAIN

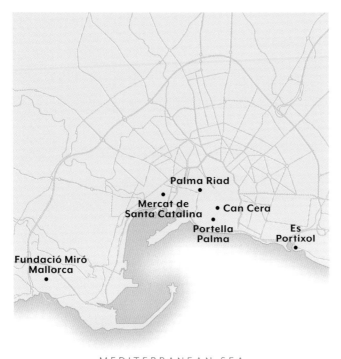

Palma Riad

Mercat de
Santa Catalina

Can Cera

Portella
Palma

Es
Portixol

Fundació Miró
Mallorca

MEDITERRANEAN SEA

highlights

1 / Dive into the world of Catalan artist Joan Miró; the unmissable **Fundació Miró Mallorca** includes two studios, Son Boter and Taller Sert.

2 / Stay in a soulfully converted historic building, such as **Palma Riad**, **Portella Palma** or **Can Cera**.

3 / Join a two-wheel city tour or rent a bike and cycle along the seafront to Es Portixol.

4 / Wander around the buzzy **Mercat de Santa Catalina**, then stop for tapas and vermouth at market counter **Can Frau** or enjoy a meal in this food-loving district.

With its flourishing food scene, simmering creative energy and unmissable art collections, Palma is redefining the idea of a sunny Balearic Islands break and making a name for itself as a stylish, culture-focused, year-round destination. For 2025, Mallorca's Med-hugging capital promises the launch of a long-awaited, green-driven waterfront promenade to explore on foot or by bike. Meanwhile, design-led heritage-building hotels, fresh-faced independent galleries and some of Spain's most exciting new restaurants continue to pop up around its ancient streets, particularly in the Old Town and Santa Catalina neighbourhood.

A REVITALISED WATERFRONT

Palma's much-anticipated new *paseo marítimo* (seafront promenade) is set to be unveiled in early 2025, stretching 3.5km (2.2 miles) around the bay from the southern edge of the Old Town to Porto Pí. In the works since 2022, this €60 million project will completely transform a previously traffic-heavy strip of the city's waterfront, creating a pedestrian- and cyclist-friendly haven overlooking the Mediterranean. Palm-filled gardens, outdoor seating areas, playgrounds for kids, broad pedestrian crossings, wheelchair-accessible ramps and new bike-share stations are all part of plans led by Ibiza-born architect Elías Torres, while vehicle lanes will be significantly reduced and traffic diverted elsewhere. Other planned green initiatives for Palma's fresh seafront boulevard include bringing in LED lighting, planting over 1800 trees and creating sustainable drainage systems so rain-water can be reused. For both local residents and Palma-loving visitors, it will become a refreshing place to linger, either on tree-shaded benches during warmer months or while soaking up the winter sun.

CREATIVE CULTURE

From Jorge Luis Borges (who praised Palma's spectacular cathedral in poetry) to George Sand (who lived at Valldemossa's Real Cartuja with Frédéric Chopin), Mallorca has been nurturing creative souls for many years. Palma is at the heart of the island's cultural scene, and the entire city is a treat for lovers of the arts. A slew of fabulous galleries starts with the hilltop Fundació Miró Mallorca and the Old-Town's Es Baluard, built into Palma's old walls, but there's much more. Now you're just as likely to hear (or even join) heated book-club discussions at local cafes, meet contemporary artists (both Mallorcan and

2

Palma's waterfront, overlooked by the vast Catedral de Mallorca – aka La Seu **1** Candyfloss colours in central Palma **2** Lunch alfresco, with a view of the Mallorcan hills

One of my favourite literary corners in Palma is El Terreno district. Wandering its steep narrow streets we follow in the footsteps of such authors as Gertrude Stein, DH Lawrence and Camilo José Cela.

MARINA ALONSO DE CASO
/ Founder of La Salina bookshop, Santa Catalina

international) at their new Palma studios or stumble across boutiques devoted to continuing centuries of tradition in local crafts. Then there's the annual Nit de l'Art (Art Night), which sees exhibitions and performances take over Palma's historic centre and is due to celebrate its 29th edition in September 2025.

All this creativity is also spilling over into a crop of boutique hotels that are busy reviving ancient heritage buildings as magical, design-forward places to stay, where the focus is on Mallorca-made art, local artisanal crafts and warm Mediterranean light.

LOCAL FOOD SCENE

The last few years have seen Palma step into Spain's gastronomic spotlight, but anyone who already loves the capital will know that eating and drinking here is a joy. Whether you fancy a simple *tostada* (toast) topped with local *sobrassada* (spiced sausage), a sugary *ensaïmada* (pastry) to go with coffee or a high-cuisine Mallorca-inspired tasting menu, Palma now happily rivals Spain's other food capitals. Seasonal, locally grown, often-organic produce is a big part of the

5

secret here, provided by *fincas* (estates) all over the island and lively urban markets where chefs shop for the day's ingredients. Some of the hottest new restaurants are opening up in the arty Santa Catalina district (just west of the Old Town), where the energetic neighbourhood market now mingles with a lineup of creative kitchens overseen by adventurous globally trained chefs. And of 16 Michelin-starred options dotted across the Balearics in 2024, four of them are in Palma. It's all celebrated during the increasingly popular TaPalma tapas festival, which usually happens every November.

3 Castell de Bellver, delivering head-turning views of the city and the Badia de Palma **4** Stop off at a Palma *pastelería* to pick up sugary treats like local *ensaïmada* **5** Outdoor dining on the Paseo Sagrera

when to go

Palma is a wonderful year-round destination, and savvy travellers are now tapping into the many joys of off-season travel here. Skip the peak-summer months (July and August), when prices and crowds skyrocket.

how to get there

Palma de Mallorca Airport has flights to/from destinations all over Europe, as well as seasonal links with Newark in the US. Time permitting, it's also possible to catch the ferry to Palma from several transport hubs in mainland Spain, including Barcelona, Valencia and Dénia. The Barcelona–Palma journey, for example, takes 6½ to 7½ hours.

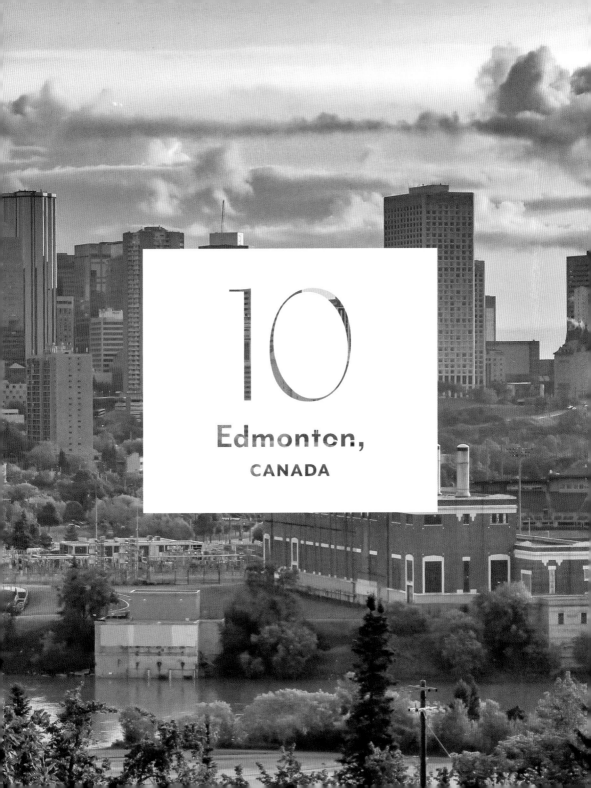

10
Edmonton,
CANADA

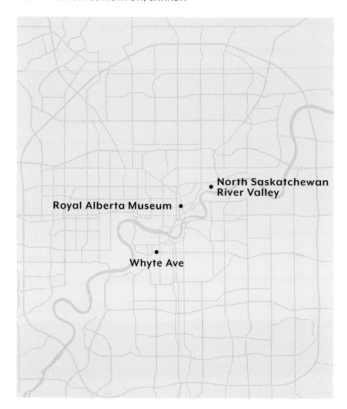

highlights

1 / Join the **Edmonton International Fringe Festival** for 11 days of live shows in parks, small theatres and on the streets.

2 / Enjoy arts, boutique shopping and multicultural food on **Whyte Ave**, the main artery of the Old Strathcona neighbourhood.

3 / Head into nature in **North Saskatchewan River Valley**, Edmonton's substantial urban parkland which fans out in a huge interconnected green belt beside the river, replete with lakes, bridges, ravines and trails.

4 / Peruse the province's natural and cultural history at the **Royal Alberta Museum**, western Canada's largest, refreshed and relocated in 2018.

If you haven't been to Edmonton in the last 10 years, prepare yourself for a double-take. Canada's fifth-largest city has long been celebrated for its legendary fringe festival and bohemian Old Strathcona district, but in recent times Herculean efforts have been put into revitalising its once lacklustre downtown with sleek skyscrapers and state-of-the-art sports and entertainment facilities. In an era of truth and reconciliation, the city has also responded to a surge of interest in Indigenous culture with engrossing immersive experiences at places like Fort Edmonton and out-of-town Métis Crossing.

DOWNTOWN REBIRTH

Billions of dollars have been poured into the regeneration of Edmonton's downtown over the last decade, with whole neighbourhoods being reshaped. Leading the way is the Ice District, previously an amalgam of vacant buildings and half-empty car parks that has been transformed into the second-largest sports and entertainment district in North America. Ground zero for sports and music fans is Rogers Place, a 20,734-capacity indoor arena whose futuristic curvilinear structure sits alongside a deluxe JW Marriott hotel and the 250m-high (820ft) Stantec Tower, Edmonton's tallest structure to date. From the musical sphere, Rogers draws the likes of Drake and Paul McCartney; sports-wise, it's home to iconic National Hockey League team, the Oilers. Seeing the beloved Oilers battle pugnaciously on the ice remains an Edmonton rite of passage. It's nearly four decades since the team won an astonishing five Stanley Cups in seven years led by a certain Wayne Gretzky, alias the 'Great One', but with a side currently inspired by the man popularly considered to be the world's finest player, Connor McDavid, they have reemerged as potential contenders, cheered on by famously fanatical supporters. Who knows, 2025 could be their year.

BECOME A FAN

The Ice District's most recent addition is the so-called 'Fan Park', built on the site of a demolished casino. A year-round activity hub, the multi-use space hosts a snow maze, ice slides and skating rink in the winter, and festivals like Sustainival and Rock the District in the summer.

Expanding east, the urban revitalisation has recently spilled over into Station Lands, where new residential units are seeking to

Edmonton's soaring skyline **1** Dusk over downtown Edmonton **2** The city's Neon Sign Museum, a collection of restored retro pieces adorning the walls along the 4th St Promenade

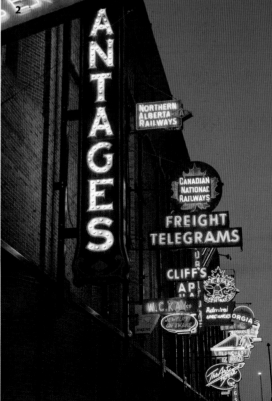

Discover mom and pop gems in Chinatown, rent e-bikes in Old Strathcona to zip around North America's largest stretch of urban river valley parkland, or visit during festival season – which is year-round!

LINDA HOANG
/ Social media strategist

attract young professionals and make downtown more attractive and liveable. In 2023, Edmonton set up a vibrancy fund to support city centre activities and festivals, spearheaded by a 'Meet me in downtown' marketing campaign. The long-term plan is to make the city core more walkable, bikeable and transit friendly. Kickstarting that process, the LRT (Light Rail Transit) network opened the new Valley Line in November 2023, with 16 more stations planned by 2026.

INDIGENOUS IMPETUS

Stoked by a growing interest in conservation and cultural reconnection, Alberta's Indigenous communities have developed more opportunities for tourists to learn about their history, traditions and culture. Background info can be gleaned at the Royal Alberta Museum's Human History Hall, while Fort Edmonton Park's engaging Indigenous Peoples Experience was enhanced by a special storytelling series in 2024.

Using the city as a base, it's well worth driving 80 minutes north to Métis Crossing on the banks of the North Saskatchewan River. Occupying 200 hectares (500 acres) of farmland owned by Métis settlers (people

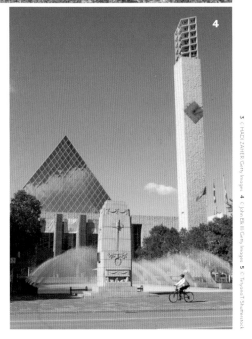

5

of mixed European and Indigenous ancestry) since the late 1800s, a new cultural gathering centre and high-end lodge offer overnight stays and tours. The latter focus on music, dance, traditional home life and the reintroduction of native wildlife species, including white bison and elk. Accommodation is in a Métis-designed boutique hotel whose plush rooms have recently been complemented by deluxe star-watching domes equipped with transparent ceilings, heated floors and king-size beds designed for viewing the aurora borealis.

3 Autumn leaves paint the parklands of North Saskatchewan River Valley **4** Edmonton's Friendship Tower and City Hall **5** Downtown Edmonton, hugged by the curving North Saskatchewan River

when to go

As Edmonton's winters can be brutally cold, summer is the best time to visit. The International Fringe Festival is held in August.

how to get there

Most people fly into Edmonton International Airport, which has good links to US and other Canadian cities. From outside North America, you can connect through Toronto or Vancouver. Calgary is a three-hour drive to the south; Red Arrow runs daily buses.

further reading

The Battle of Alberta: the Historic Rivalry Between the Edmonton Oilers and the Calgary Flames, by Mark Spector, emphasises the importance of hockey to Edmontonians.

BEST in TRAVEL 2025

TOP
10
REGIONS

01 South Carolina's Lowcountry & Coastal Georgia, USA / 02 The Terai, Nepal / 03 Chiriquí, Panama / 04 Launceston & the Tamar Valley, Australia / 05 Valais, Switzerland / 06 Giresun & Ordu, Türkiye / 07 Bavaria, Germany / 08 East Anglia, England / 09 Jordan Trail / 10 Mt Hood & the Columbia River Gorge, USA

01

South Carolina's
LOWCOUNTRY &
COASTAL GEORGIA, USA

Columbia

Augusta

Charleston • **City Market**

Haunted Squares
Savannah •**Savannah Bananas**

S A R G A S S O
S E A

Brunswick

• **Cumberland Island**

highlights

1 / Spend the afternoon strolling Savannah's **Starland District**, taking in street murals, vintage shops and bohemian cafes.

2 / Go gallery hopping in Charleston's cobblestoned **French Quarter**, then return by night for a performance at the historic Dock Street Theatre.

3 / Learn about the lives of enslaved people touring a Gullah cemetery and former dwelling on the 19th-century **McLeod Plantation**.

4 / Look for dolphins on a sunrise walk along Hilton Head Island's **Coligny Beach**, then have a hearty breakfast at **Lowcountry Produce Market & Café**.

O n a road trip through South Carolina's and Georgia's Lowcountry, you'll encounter golden beaches, windswept marshes and old-fashioned towns seemingly unchanged by the passage of time. But underneath the tranquil facade lies a surprising dynamism. Led by the historic cities of Savannah and Charleston, the region has become one of America's trailblazers when it comes to sustainable energy. Its culinary scene has taken an outsized share of top awards thanks to a new crop of innovative chefs, and some much-needed soul searching has resulted in it now being home to one of the nation's best African-American museums.

FACING THE PAST, DREAMING OF A BRIGHTER FUTURE

Until recently, the Lowcountry struggled to address its troubled history connected with enslavement. Today, Charleston's former pier – where thousands of kidnapped Africans were sold into slavery – has been transformed into one of the most important museums in the south, the International African American Museum. Thought-provoking galleries take visitors on a journey from ancient Africa to the present day, with exhibitions on the Black Atlantic world linking Africa, Europe and the Americas. The museum also shines a light on the Gullah Geechee (Lowcountry descendants of enslaved people), and its cultural programme is a vital draw for both locals and out-of-towners, with drumming workshops, film screenings and live performances.

The area surrounding the museum – which sits on pilings above infamous Gadsden's Wharf where around 100,000 enslaved Africans arrived – has been christened the African Ancestors Memorial Garden. Etched on the ground, silhouetted figures represent those imprisoned in a ship's hold, while kneeling figures commemorate those who died here. The garden's greenery blends two disparate worlds, with African palms growing above sweetgrass native to South Carolina.

GREEN ENERGY, GREENER LANDSCAPES

Savannah is burnishing its green credentials, with the goal of meeting 30% of its power needs by clean, renewable energy in 2025. West of town, a new electric vehicle plant – costing a whopping US$4.3 billion – will start producing an estimated 300,000 cars this year in one of the biggest projects of its kind in the USA. Thousands of new jobs will add to the economic boom that the region is already experiencing.

Wooden docks on the Savannah marshlands **1** Charleston's Rainbow Row, a terrace of candy coloured Georgian houses on East Bay St **2** Lowcountry coastline on Hilton Head Island

> I moved to Savannah to live in a historic city with great parks for walking, running and enjoying the outdoors. I also love being close to the beach – lovely Tybee Island is less than 30 minutes away.
>
> **RACHEL SEELEY**
> / Athletic trainer

The Lowcountry was already famous for its leafy parks and elegant promenades lined with Spanish moss-draped live oaks, but when it comes to green spaces, you can never have too many. Charleston's American Gardens open in 2025 off Meeting St in the historic district, with a lane of crepe myrtles, a bubbling fountain and a small stage for mini-concerts, literary events and film screenings. Similarly, Hilton Head, just up the coast, is busily adding new green spaces, including the Patterson Family Park, featuring an innovative farm-inspired playground, as well as Gullah poetry, murals and old stories written on park structures.

GREEN ENERGY, GREENER LANDSCAPES

Food plays a starring role in any visit to the Lowcountry. New restaurants sprout like wildflowers, and the region's eating options featured prominently on a recent list of semifinalists for the James Beard Foundation Awards. The Obstinate Daughter's Jaques Larson, nominated for best chef of the year, continues to wow diners with his innovative blend of European-inflected Southern dishes, served up by the shore on Sullivan's Island.

3 © zorzamora Shutterstock 4 © Daniela Duncan Getty Images 5 © SeanPavonePhoto Getty Images

Charleston and Savannah are both packed with celebrated spots such as the latter's Cotton & Rye, named by *USA Today* as one of the country's best restaurants. And these days, you'll also find plenty of great dining outside the cities, from rustic spots like Lowcountry Fish Camp in Summerville (with mouth-watering plates of blackened catfish) to Okàn in Bluffton, where award-winning chef Bernard Bennett takes you on a culinary expedition through West Africa, the Caribbean and the South Carolina Coast.

3 Savour Southern flavours in classic dishes like a Lowcountry boil, fusing shrimp, spicy sausage and potatoes **4** Statuary in Savannah's serene Bonaventure Cemetery **5** Spanish moss drapes the live oaks around Forsyth Park's fountain, Savannah

when to go

Heat and humidity soar during the summer, which is also prime hurricane season. Come in the early spring for more pleasant temperatures and ample celebrations, including the Savannah Music Festival.

how to get there

Savannah/Hilton Head Airport and Charleston Airport have flights to destinations on the East Coast and in the Midwest. More scenic is arriving by Amtrak train, which connects both cities with Washington (DC), Jacksonville (Florida) and points in between.

further reading

Dr Jessica Berry's *The Little Gullah Geechee Book* provides a fascinating introduction to Lowcountry traditions, cuisine, language and spiritual beliefs. *Slavery and Freedom in Savannah* features essays by a dozen different writers on Black life from the city's founding to the 20th century.

02

The Terai,
NEPAL

epal is synonymous with the Himalaya, yet the southern lowlands – a ribbon of forests, grasslands and wetlands known as the Terai – showcase a completely different side to the country. Covering a quarter of its landmass, this underappreciated region is a biodiversity hotspot, its reserves renowned for their rhinos and birdlife. The Terai is culturally rich too, home to one of the world's most important Buddhist sites, a glorious Hindu temple and an overlooked tea-growing centre. And aside from a handful of destinations – notably Chitwan National Park – it's still easy to escape the crowds.

LAND OF THE ONE-HORNED RHINO

Originally a royal hunting ground before being transformed into a wildlife reserve, Chitwan National Park played a vital role in saving the greater one-horned rhino from the brink of extinction. The UNESCO World Heritage Site – the Terai's

highlights

1 / Take a canoe or boat safari along **Chitwan's Rapti River**, keeping your eyes peeled for rhinos and huge gharial crocodiles.

2 / Look round **Lumbini's Maya Devi** temple, which marks the birthplace of the Buddha.

3 / Visit the **Janakpur Women's Development Centre**, an NGO that helps local women to keep traditional Mithila arts and crafts traditions alive.

4 / Enjoy a tasting session and help out with the harvest on a tour of one of **Ilam's tea gardens**.

biggest tourist attraction – now has an estimated 694 of these majestic creatures, almost a fifth of the total population. Numbers are growing here and, as a result, sightings are common on jeep, walking, canoe and boat safaris. You're also likely to encounter an array of other species, from sloth bears and gharial crocodiles to elephants and – if you're lucky – tigers. And the conservation work continues – rare smooth-coated otters were recently spotted in the park for the first time in two decades.

To the west, Bardiya National Park is quieter than Chitwan, but equally beguiling. The Terai's largest protected area is a seemingly untouched realm of forests, savannah and rivers stalked by a rising tiger population – 125 big cats as of 2022 – as well as around 38 rhinos. Two of the latter have also recently been introduced to the bird-watching haven of Koshi Tappu, a previously rhino-less wildlife reserve in the wetlands of the eastern Terai. The youngsters – rescued by conservationists after being abandoned as calves – join hundreds of avian species, as well as the last surviving group of endangered wild water buffalo in Nepal.

TEA & ENLIGHTENMENT

The Terai also boasts two of Nepal's most important religious sites, both of which draw pilgrims from across South Asia and beyond, but relatively few travellers.

The Terai's Chitwan National Park, home of the one-horned rhino and one of the premier drawcards in all of Nepal **1** Raise your eyes to the skies in Bardiya National Park to see spectacular species like the purple sunbird **2** Harvesting tea in Ilam

Chitwan's popularity has always dwarfed Bardiya's, but this 'Wild Wild West' on the southwestern plains of the Terai is the place to be for travellers and wildlife enthusiasts seeking experiences of the other side of Nepal.

ABHI SHRESTHA
/ CEO of Rural Heritage/Snow Cat Travel

Surrounded by meditative gardens, the Maya Devi temple in Lumbini marks the spot where Siddhartha Gautama – aka the Buddha – was born in around 563 BCE. The structure is one of the country's foremost archaeological sites, as well as a place of immense spiritual significance. It sits in a vast, tranquil park dotted with modern temples and monasteries – whose diverse styles reflect the architectural traditions of Buddhist communities around the world – as well as the gleaming gold-and-white Shanti Stupa (Peace Pagoda).

Some 300km (186 miles) east of Lumbini, the centrepiece of the sacred city of Janakpur is the eye-catching Janaki Mandir, a Hindu temple completed in 1910. Dedicated to the goddess Sita, who is said to have been found on the site as an infant, it is particularly evocative at night when illuminated by glittering multi-coloured lights. Janakpur is also the hub of a revived folk art tradition, Mithila painting, which dates back almost three millennia.

For a change of scene, continue to the far eastern reaches of the Terai, where the tea-growing area of Ilam receives only

3

4

a fraction of the tourists compared to its better-known counterpart Darjeeling, which lies just across the nearby Indian border. Accessed via a serpentine road, Ilam's lush green hills are blanketed with tea gardens, several of which offer tours and tastings – the best time to visit is during the April-to-November picking season. Beyond top-notch chai, Ilam's valleys, ridges and forests of pine, oak and rhododendron are contemplative spots for hiking and birdwatching.

when to go

The Terai is best visited from late September to the pre-monsoon period, which typically begins in mid-April; avoid the monsoon (roughly mid-June to mid-September) itself.

how to get there

Regular buses link the Terai's main cities and towns with Kathmandu and Pokhara; tourist buses also run to/from Chitwan. There are several airports in the region and four border crossings with India.

further reading

Soul of the Rhino is an insightful account of efforts to prevent the extinction of rhinos in Nepal by leading conservationist Hemanta Mishra, while *Karnali Blues* is a bestselling novel about a father-son relationship by Terai-born author and journalist Buddhisagar.

3 Chestnut-headed bee-eaters in the forests of Bardiya National Park 4 Janakpur's pilgrim-thronged Janaki Mandir 5 Tarai gray langur in the Terai lowlands 6 Maya Devi Temple in Lumbini, sacred birthplace of the Buddha

03

Chiriquí,
PANAMA

PACIFIC OCEAN | Montuosa Island & Hannibal Bank (65 km/40 miles)

Panama has long captivated travellers thanks to the engineering marvel that is its famous canal, and the idyllic Bocas del Toro archipelago in the Caribbean. Less known is the province of Chiriquí, in the far west, where you can enjoy a healthy ecosystem, explore cloud forests and coffee plantations, climb volcanoes and lounge on Pacific islands in a national marine park. For bird enthusiasts, the country offers the opportunity to observe over a thousand species – the most iconic of which is the quetzal, revered as a sacred symbol by the Maya and Aztecs.

DISCOVER NEW TRAILS

Situated at the westernmost edge of the country, the province of Chiriquí boasts astounding biodiversity and burgeoning options for hiking, coffee tours, boat trips and snorkeling within the pristine surroundings of the Gulf of

highlights

1 / Make the charming, riverside town of **Boquete** your starting point for activities in the province of Chiriquí.

2 / Be wowed by **Finca Drácula** if you're a flower lover, a botanical garden holding more than 2000 types of orchids, one of the largest collections in the world.

3 / Fish for kingfish, tuna and dorado, among other species, at popular angling destinations like **Hannibal Bank** and Montuosa island.

4 / Get wet and wild rafting the white waters of **Chiriquí Viejo River**.

Chiriquí. The region's meticulously maintained environment provides a remote escape for nature enthusiasts in places like Mt Totumas Cloud Forest, a 162-hectare (400 acres) preserve that continually expands its network of trails. Getting there is no easy feat, but the journey is well worth it. Access is limited to 4WD pickup trucks which have to navigate a challenging 9km (5.5 miles) rocky road. Once there, head deep into the cloud forest for birdwatching – the recorded count exceeds 280 species – and the chance to hear the distant calls of howler monkeys. Recently inaugurated trails extend over 30km (19 miles) and are perfect for exploring, particularly from January to May when the quetzal is most visible. Other sites, like the Tamandúa Reserve, also offer birdwatching experiences and specialised tours aimed at photographers.

ISLAND ADVENTURES & COFFEE KICKS

Gulf of Chiriquí National Marine Park comprises a series of islands and mangroves stretching across 150km (93 miles). Embarking on a boat tour here is a delightful way to visit local communities and discover their products, such as cocoa, while keeping an eye out for whales en route. One of the islands, Bolaños, is an incredible spot for snorkelling – it has extensive reefs – while Gamez Island is of volcanic origin and full of almond and palm trees.

Chasing waterfalls in the Chiriquí cloud forest **1** Take a guided hike into Mt Totumas Cloud Forest to spot the resplendent quetzal **2** Explore natural treasures around Boquete like the Lost Waterfalls (aka Las Tres Cascadas)

> In Panama, nature is pristine. It creates a favourable environment because we are all happy to be here. The country boasts a remarkably healthy ecosystem, and our collective responsibility is to preserve and care for it.

JEFFREY DIETRICH
/ Owner of Mount Totumas
  Cloud Forest and Biological Reserve

3

4

Back on land, Don Pepe Estate Coffee offers a captivating look at one of the main crops grown in Chiriquí. Nestled in the foothills of the Barú volcano, the estate is an immersive introduction to the world of coffee. The farm produces seven varieties on a small scale, among them the geisha variety, known as the most expensive coffee in the world – in Panama, half a kilo (just over 1lb) sells for about US$350. The whole process is explained on the tour by knowledgeable and entertaining guide Carlos Antonio Jurado, and the visit ends with a tasting.

An hour's drive from Don Pepe, Volcán Barú National Park presents an exhilarating challenge for hikers who love lengthy, strenuous trails. This imposing, dormant volcano is the highest point in Panama, reaching 3474m (11,398ft), and the ascent along the route is rigorous, taking six to eight hours and requiring a guide. The landscape

5

6

undergoes a mesmerising transformation as you walk, changing from humid mountains to low forests. From the summit, you can see both the Atlantic and Pacific Oceans at the same time. If all that hiking sounds just too much, save your legs and take a vehicle to the summit in a 90-minute trip. However you get to the top, sunset above the clouds and stargazing are experiences you will long remember.

3 Strawberry specialties at Fresas Café **4** Ripening coffee berries on a plantation near Boquete **5** Spot distictive keel-billed toucans in Chiriquí's lush mountains and lowlands **6** Discover a technicolour underwater world in the Gulf of Chiriquí National Marine Park

when to go

It's possible to visit Chiriquí all year round. Birdwatching is best January-April. The vegetation is lush and intense during the rainy season (May-December). The humpback whale season is from June to October, but you can see dolphins throughout the year.

how to get there

The best way to get to Chiriquí is by flying from Panama City to the small airport in David. Boca Chica is the ideal hub for exploring and discovering the wonders of the Gulf of Chiriquí National Marine Park. Local companies provide boat trips to several captivating islands.

04

Launceston & THE
TAMAR VALLEY, AUSTRALIA

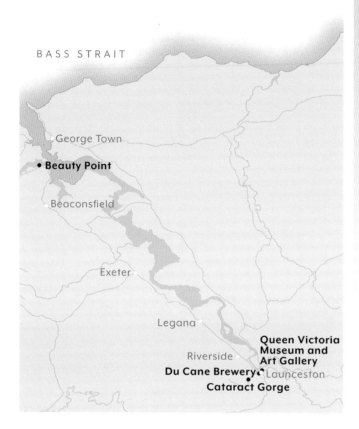

BASS STRAIT

George Town

• **Beauty Point**

Beaconsfield

Exeter

Legana

Riverside

Queen Victoria Museum and Art Gallery

Du Cane Brewery · Launceston

Cataract Gorge

highlights

1 / Thread through **Cataract Gorge** on walking trails, peer down onto peacocks and wallabies from the chairlift, or dine in style at Gorge Restaurant.

2 / Learn the sad story of Tasmania's tragic thylacine and peruse the likes of bushrangers' (criminals in the 18th and 19th centuries) guns and a planetarium at **QVMAG**, Australia's largest regional museum.

3 / Head downstream to **Beauty Point**, viewing platypuses and wandering among feeding echidnas at Platypus House. Want more animals? Seahorse World is right next door.

4 / Plot your Tasmanian bushwalks on the maps that cover the cavernous walls of **Du Cane**, Launceston's first craft brewery.

It's Tasmania's second city and Australia's second City of Gastronomy (along with Bendigo in Victoria), but Launceston lives in the shadow of no place. At the edge of the fertile volcanic plains that nourish Tasmania's reputation for gourmet goodness, and with the state's prime wine region all but wrapped around its edges, Launceston is a happy marriage of nature and nurture – step out of deep, craggy Cataract Gorge, which runs almost into the city centre, and it's all about wining and dining.

FERMENTING A REPUTATION

While the art juggernaut of Museum of Old and New Art (Mona) and the winter fun of the Dark Mofo festival elevated the profile of Tasmania's capital Hobart, Launceston quietly worked on its cool. Furnished with a rich collection of 19th-century industrial architecture, and located where the North and South Esk Rivers fight through gorges to become kanamaluka/River Tamar, 'Lonnie', as the locals affectionately call it, already had myriad outdoor destinations by day and places to feed you royally at night. Then, in 2021, Launceston was named a UNESCO City of Gastronomy, joining a select table of the now 50 belly-rubbing destinations around the world. It's international recognition that this small city of 77,000 people is a hive of quality produce, fine restaurants and a swathe of wineries. In 2025 the city's focus will go even more intently onto food, with the anticipated opening of the Fermentation Hub on its northern edge. Planned as a space and support for start-up fermentation businesses, this world-first centre will cover everything from cheeses and cider to pickles and beer, with public areas allowing visitors to see the fermentation process up close.

TEMPTATIONS IN EVERY DIRECTION

Whether you drive north or south of Launceston, you hit a Tamar Valley cellar door within 12 km (7 miles) of the city centre. The state's oldest and largest wine region spills across both banks of kanamaluka/River Tamar and contains more than 30 vineyards that can be strung together on the Tamar Valley Wine Route. One of the pioneering vignerons, Andrew Pirie, is still here at appointment-only Apogee, while a visit to House of Arras will put you in the company of the wine named world's best

The Tamar Valley's famed Pinot Noir grapes, ripening on the vine **1** Alexandra Suspension Bridge in Launceston's Cataract Gorge **2** Sample delectable Tasmanian produce, from freshly shucked local oysters to Lonnie-made cheeses

3. © Ness Vanderburgh/Tourism Tasmania

What I love about Lonnie is that it's a city that's really just a big country town, with heaps of hidden gems. Favourite watering holes are Havilah wine bar and Saint John Craft Beer.

RHYS HANNAN
/ Market manager, Harvest Launceston

sparkling by Decanter Magazine in 2020. Just as famous is Nellie, Swinging Gate Vineyard's Staffy, once the cover girl on a book about winery dogs.

Food miles in Launceston are minimal, with one of Australia's most fertile farming areas immediately to the city's west, cultivating the likes of the country's first black truffles along with menus worth of prime beef and vegetables. Much of this produce comes fresh to the city on Saturday mornings at Harvest Launceston, a car-park farmers market with stalls staffed by the growers and makers themselves.

NATURE RULES

A fifteen-minute walk from Launceston is the mouth of scenic Cataract Gorge. Beneath its sheer dolerite walls, the 5km (3 miles) gorge briefly opens up at First Basin, where lawns sport a riverside swimming pool and the world's longest single-span chairlift.

There's more outdoor beauty within an hour's drive of the city, including an abundance of wildlife, mountain biking and Tasmania's best skiing. Beach-lined Narawntapu National Park has been dubbed the 'Serengeti of Australia' for its mass of wallabies and other critters, while little penguins march ashore nightly, right

Restaurants Around Launceston

1 / **Stillwater:** Lonnie's stalwart dining room, delivering locally accented menus inside an 1830 flour mill by Cataract Gorge.

2 / **Black Cow Bistro:** Carnivores, saddle up at this ode to Tasmanian beef, from Cape Grim to Robbins Island wagyu.

3 / **Stelo at Pierre's:** In appearance it's part Parisian cafe and part bordello, but Stelo is adamant about local produce, with Italian twists.

4 / **Timbre Kitchen:** Slip in among the vines at Velo Wines for a daily-changing menu of Tasmanian flavours.

5 / **Josef Chromy Wines:** You've barely left Launceston when you hit the vines at Josef Chromy's delectable winery restaurant.

past the toes of visitors, near the mouth of kanamaluka/River Tamar at Low Head. Nearby George Town features the newest of Tasmania's burgeoning mountain-bike trail networks, while Ben Lomond National Park to the south contains the state's second-highest peak (Legges Tor) and a low-key ski field. Snow conditions aren't reliable, but even if there's no white stuff, the road up, along serpentine Jacob's Ladder, is one of the most dramatic drives in Australia.

3 Discover Tasmanian flavours on a deep dive into the Launceston restaurant scene **4** Engage with echidnas at Beauty Point's Platypus House **5** Keep your food miles low with a feast of local produce, from Tasmanian truffles to locally reared beef

when to go

As a city of long winters, Launceston embraces summer with relish, turning on a string of festivals. The three-day, food-focussed Festivale is arguably the local favourite. The Launceston BeerFest rings in the new year, and the satellite town of Evandale hosts the National Penny Farthing Championships, which roll nostalgically through the town in February, followed by Australia's richest prize for landscape painting, the Glover Prize.

how to get there

There are direct flights to Launceston from all Australian mainland state capitals.

05

Valais,
SWITZERLAND

LAKE
GENEVA

Monthey

Sion

• **Aletsch Glacier**

Brig

Martigny

• **Pierre Avoi**
• **Le Châble**

FRANCE

Zermatt

ITALY

• **Klein Matterhorn**

Verbier, Zermatt, and the bewitching Matterhorn with its unfathomable trigonometry: certain icons need no introduction in this region of Switzerland, where English aristocrats stopped on their Grand Tour of Europe during the 19th century and millennial starlets quaff champagne cocktails in some of the world's glitziest ski resorts today. Yet beneath the blatant glamour there lies a trove of rich and timeless pastoral tradition – as enduringly steadfast as the region's 2025 drive to blaze electrifying new trails.

ROCKY FLOWS, FOREST JUMPS & GNARLY DOWNHILLS

Verbier resort, in the Lower Valais, has been a byword for world-class skiing (and more recently, freeriding) since the 1950s, when the first of now-90-plus lifts went in. But it's the explosive mountain-biking scene that is the real heart

highlights

1 / Ride three cable cars from **Zermatt to Klein Matterhorn** to spot 14 glaciers and 30-plus peaks above 4000m (13,123ft).

2 / Taste **raclette** by artisan producers at Le Châble's two-day cheese fest Bagnes Capitale de la Raclette.

3 / Experience Verbier from a new angle: summit **Pierre Avoi** and hike along centuries-old *bisses* (waterways) built to irrigate pastures.

4 / Explore the **Aletsch Glacier**, the Alps' largest sea of ice, on a guided summer glacier hike or winter ski-touring expedition from Fiesch.

stealer. In summer 2025 the region hosts the UCI World Mountain Bike Championships, with the opening ceremony firing up the quiet town of Sion, 55km (34 miles) from Verbier, and biking events unfurling in seven surrounding mountain resorts. Notably, these world champs will bring together seven disciplines for the first time, including e-mountain biking. The fastest-growing market in the Alps right now, electric-powered mountain biking was valued at US$5.77 billion globally in 2024 and is expected to double within five years. Walk down Verbier's main street, Rue de Médran, on a spring day and you might well feel underdressed, such is the throng of protection-clad bikers heading to the Médran gondola to be whisked up the mountain with their wheels. In Les Ruinettes, at 2200m (7218ft), bikers tear down 19km (12 miles) of tracks in Verbier Bike Park: trails range from beginner-gentle to fly-by-the-seat-of-your-pants vertical – it's not for nothing that the official competition track is named Tire's Fire. All this and celestial views of the Massif des Combins and Mont Blanc too. More mapped e-bike itineraries, encouraging scenic cruising for all abilities, and August's ramped-up Verbier E-Bike Festival, pairing e-biking with gourmet snacking and music, are part of the Valais' 2025 campaign to move mountain biking from niche to mainstream – and encourage more young riders and women to blaze trails.

Grand views from Zermatt's Gornergrat train **1** The mighty Matterhorn, framed by Zermatt's cable cars **2** Move over, skiing: mountain biking is taking off in the Valais

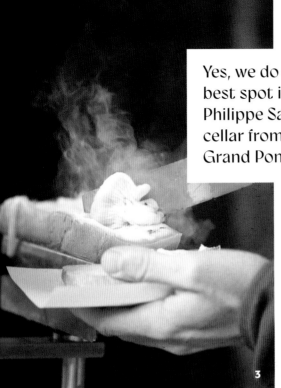

Yes, we do eat raclette in summer too! The best spot in Sion is the Friday market or Philippe Savioz' Cave Les Futailles, a wine cellar from the 13th century on Rue du Grand Pont.

SABINE DE KALBERMATTEN-VAN VLIET
/ Valais native

BACK TO GRASSROOTS BASICS

It's no coincidence that the Championships' marathon event will wind through Val d'Anniviers, a clandestine side valley brushed with pines and storybook villages of dark-timber granaries on stilts and whitewashed chapels. This is the hushed yang to the Valais' exuberant, jet-set yin: the unsung heritage soul of the region where traditional rye bread is still baked in the communal *four à pain* (oven) and families store rounds of 'death cheese' in the cellar to crack open at funerals. Climb up to the villages of St Luc, Grimentz and Zinal by e-bike and enjoy corkscrewing through an alpine tableau yet to be discovered by the crowds. Amid the intoxicating flush of 4000m (13,120 ft)-plus-peaks on the horizon, spot the iconic Matterhorn. To stride out further, consider Valais Alpine Bike, a new 316km (196 miles), seven-stage, multi-day biking itinerary around the entire region, ending in Val d'Anniviers.

5

6

ON THE PILGRIM TRAIL

Time spent in Martigny, Valais' French-speaking capital and oldest town, quickly reveals why wine-loving Romans lingered here en route across the Col du Grand St Bernard mountain pass from Italy. In 2025, the Barryland breeding centre, home to St Bernard dogs used to rescue lost souls in the snow until the 1950s, will be upgraded to a swanky new theme park, with a floor plan inspired by a dog's pawprint. Indulge in cuddles galore on a dog walk – around Martigny in spring, through wildflower meadows on Col du Grand St Bernard in summer and along the frozen fairy-tale shores of Champex-Lac in winter.

3 Meltingly marvellous raclette, perfect sustenance after a day riding or skiing the slopes **4** Get the lowdown on the Aletsch Glacier at the Villa Cassel visitor centre on Riederalp **5** Sunrise on the Matterhorn **6** Meet and greet St Bernard dogs at Martigny's refurbished Barryland

when to go

Bikers burn flow trails March to October; from June, cable cars and chairlifts transport visitors and wheels up mountainsides (July and August in smaller resorts).

how to get there

By train or plane to Geneva, and onwards by SBB train; buy tickets online or via the SBB app. In Verbier, Médran Sports rents wheels (mountain bike, road, downhill, enduro, e-bike); Singletrail and École Suisse de VTT are recommended bike schools with guides.

further reading

Slow Train to Switzerland by Diccon Bewes is a modern-day version of the first 'London to Lucerne' package tour by train, bus and boat.

06

Giresun & Ordu,
TÜRKIYE

Giresun and Ordu, two neighbouring cities and eponymous provinces on Türkiye's Black Sea coast, are small and charming destinations where natural beauty in multiple shades of green is waiting to be discovered. From their unique beaches to the endless plateaus in the mountains above the towns, these seaside siblings offer charm, delicacies and fresh air. The warm hospitality and cultural diversity of the friendly people of the regions just add to the appeal, ensuring you have a terrific time while exploring.

PLATEAU FUN

Summer festivals, large and small, are held on the high *yaylas* (plateaus) in different districts of Ordu Province. These are cultural events in which both residents and visitors come together to indulge in regional traditions. Some last a single day, while others last several days. Perşembe, Aybastı, Korgan, Düzoba and Çambaşı Plateau festivals

highlights

1 / Taste the world's most delicious *fındık* (hazelnuts) and hazelnut paste in Giresun.

2 / Try the famous, mouth-watering **Görele *pide*** (Turkish-style pizza).

3 / Visit the **Mavi Göl** (Blue Lake) in the middle of the verdant countryside that turns turquoise, especially in the summer months.

4 / Visit **Yason Burnu**, which features a historical church and a white lighthouse overlooking the Black Sea.

are the most popular among the many that take place. You'll always hear local melodies during the festivities, where music and dance are ever-present. You won't be able to hold yourself back while watching the high-energy moves of dancers dressed in traditional costumes, especially when it comes to the most popular dances such as *horon* and *halay*. Along with the music and dancing, the most anticipated events are the wrestling competitions, when fighters struggle fiercely on the grass to pin their opponents down as spectators cheer on their favourites. In addition, horse races are also held from time to time during some plateau festivals.

TREKKING IN MAGNIFICENT NATURE

Beyond Ordu and Giresun cities are plentiful trekking routes offering opportunities to discover the region's natural beauty. Walking enthusiasts come here throughout the year to go hiking in this elevated area. As you ascend towards the clouds, along winding roads and through deep valleys, you sometimes reach routes with densely wooded forests or encounter wide open plains. Since the region receives abundant rainfall, it's possible to see every shade of green, many types of vegetation – and maybe even a rainbow. Hiking trails are generally located at high altitudes and are covered with snow in winter, so opt for the warmer months if you plan on taking to the trails.

Up in the Ordu Province highlands on the Çambaşı Plateau **1** Ordu's cobblestoned city streets **2** Wildflowers carpet the river-cleaved hills near Görele, Giresun Province

As you travel along the coasts of Ordu and Giresun, you should fill your lungs with the scent of the Black Sea, stop by unspoilt bays, drink a cup of *çay* (tea) in a fishing village and perhaps set sail on a boat.

EMINE FATOĞLU TOPKAYA
/ Local tour guide

3 © alpaksoy/Getty Images

3

TOP FIVE
Festivals in Giresun and Ordu

1 / **Aybastı Perşembe Plateau Culture and Wrestling Festival:** The biggest festival of the region, held in the last week of July.

2 / **Mayıs Yedisi Festival:** Celebrated in May with unique rituals, concerts and dance shows.

3 / **Çambarsı Plateau Winter Festival:** A winter festival, usually in January, with concerts, snowboarding and off-road races.

4 / **Whistled Language Culture and Art Festival:** Also known Kuş Dili Festival, this is held every September in Kuşköy and is dedicated to the whistling language.

5 / **Kumru Düzoba Plateau Festival:** A cultural festival, usually in July, where wrestling, cooking competitions and concerts take place.

CULINARY TREATS

Ordu and Giresun Provinces are the most important *fındık* (hazelnut) production centres in the world, meaning hazelnuts immediately come to mind when talking about local delicacies. Ordu hazelnuts are larger and leaner, while those from Giresun are smaller and oilier. Don't forget to shop at stores selling the nuts and products made from them while walking around the cities.

Another favourite food of the region is *pide*, a Turkish-style pizza, baked in a stone oven and topped with various ingredients such as cheese, minced meat, meat or vegetables. *Pides* can come in all shapes and sizes, but the one constant when eating them is that they all taste delicious.

And finally, given you're in the Black Sea Region, it would be rude not to add *muhlama* to your culinary bucket list. This traditional favourite is made with *kolot* (a local cheese), butter, corn flour and water. It impresses you first with its colour

and appetising aroma, then with the long strands of warm, stretchy cheese, and finally with the unforgettable taste that will envelop your palate. You simply can't leave the region without experiencing this rich Turkish breakfast at a place by the seafront or up in the plateaus.

3 Don't miss a taste of *muhlama*, a cheesy local speciality
4 Traditional dress in the Black Sea region **5** Giresun's aptly named Mavi Göl (Blue Lake)

when to go

Choose spring and summer, when nature is awake and the sun is shining, rather than autumn and winter, when it often rains and can get cold.

how to get there

Ordu Giresun Airport is 20km (12 miles) from Ordu downtown and 30km (19 miles) from Giresun city centre. It receives regular flights from İstanbul, Ankara and İzmir. Both cities can also be reached by road from the regional hubs of Trabzon and Samsun.

07

Bavaria,
GERMANY

highlights

1 / Spend an evening in a **beer garden** such as Munich's Chinesischer Turm or at the Forchheimer Kellerwald.

2 / Head south to the madly popular **Neuschwanstein Castle**, Ludwig II's most iconic fairy-tale pile set among the Alps.

3 / Take an electric boat across the **Königssee** in the Berchtesgadener Land, Bavaria's prettiest Alpine corner but one with a dark Nazi legacy.

4 / Road-trip down Bavaria's west on Germany's most popular holiday route, the extremely quaint **Romantic Road**.

Uber-cool modernity versus highly valued traditions, slide-rule perfection alongside beerhall revelry, and obsessive recycling – the Free State (as Bavaria is officially called) has a distinctive but often inconsistent personality. It's also a place that has diverse physical and geographical faces, from mysterious forests to snow-capped peaks, from 21st-century Munich to half-timbered hamlets. Though traditions are celebrated, Bavaria also loves change, a fact that can be seen in its ambitious, world-leading sustainability goals. So why not make 2025 the year you discover what this often eclectic German state is all about.

OKTOBER IN SEPTEMBER

What's certain to be the same in 2025 (and whenever you visit) is that Bavaria offers the world's best beer (despite what those Czechs and Belgians might say) and you can sip it in some of the planet's most character-packed and traditional beer halls and beer gardens. And 2025 will also be the year Munich's Oktoberfest, the planet's biggest beer festival, will reach or even surpass pre-Covid levels of lager consumption and general red-faced fun. That means over six million visitors and over seven million litres of beer, as well as industrial levels of food to wash it down. In 2025, Oktoberfest starts on 20 September and runs until 5 October. Yes, the most famous festival with 'October' in its name always starts in mid-September – this is to take advantage of the better weather and longer days.

GOING UP

Heading outdoors is an integral part of any visit to Bavaria, and where better to enjoy the region's natural beauty than in its sliver of the Alps along the border with Austria. The town of Garmisch-Partenkirchen is arguably Germany's top Alpine resort with the most to do all year round, and is particularly engaging for non-skiers. Top billing must go to the rail service that climbs to the top of the country's highest mountain, the Zugspitze (2962m/9718ft), a gravity defying train that has been making this seemingly impossible journey for almost a century. When visibility is good, this is the finest view in all Bavaria. The area also has some fine hiking possibilities, the best-known of which is the narrow Partnach Gorge.

Rudy Balasko/Getty Images **1** © f.cadbou/Getty Images **2** © Belikova Oksana/Shutterstock

Mountain-set Neuschwanstein, inspiration for Disney's *Sleeping Beauty* castle **1** Oktoberfest in Munich – *prost!* **2** Reach the top of the Zugspitze by train or aerial tramway

> The best way to start your day in Munich is with a *Weisswurst* breakfast – a pair of veal sausages, a crispy pretzel, sweet mustard and a tankard of wheat beer.

JOSÉ PAVEZ
/ Munich tour guide

FUSSBALL CRAZY

Not only did Germany host football's (soccer's) European Championships in 2024, Munich's Allianz Arena is also pencilled in as the venue for the UEFA Champions League final on 31 May, 2025. The stadium is one of the world's most spectacular, its plastic-wrapped exterior able to change colour depending on who is playing inside. No doubt locals would like nothing more next May than for the stadium's illumination to blush red – home team Bayern Munich's shirt colour. That would be the (red) cherry on the cake for Germany's most successful club team who, in 2025, will be celebrating 125 years since they first toe-poked a ball into a net. The team has also been confirmed as participants in the first expanded FIFA Club World Cup in the US, an event that will no doubt be beamed into every pub and beer hall across the Free State.

3 © Yulia Furman/Shutterstock 4 © bluejayphoto/Getty Images 5 © Michael Abid/Alamy

5

THE FUTURE IS GRÜN

Bayern Munich might play in red, but most of Bavaria is most definitely green, and we're not talking just hop fields. The region has some of the most clearly defined ecological and sustainability goals on Earth, and unlike most places has the strategies and ongoing research in place to achieve them. From waste management to noise pollution, air quality control to 'electrosmog' monitoring, Bavaria doesn't just talk green, it acts green.

3 Start your day with a hearty Bavarian *Weisswurst* breakfast (and maybe a beer, too) **4** Mountain-cradled Königssee and the onion-domed St Bartholomä chapel **5** Rothenburg ob der Tauber, a medieval marvel on the Romantic Road

when to go

Any time is a good time to visit Munich. Late spring to autumn (May to October) is best for the rest of the state, December to March for Alpine snow sports.

how to get there

Munich is one of Europe's busiest airports with flight arrivals from around the world. A good alternative is Frankfurt, which has excellent transport links into Bavaria. The rail network is exemplary, and Bavaria borders Austria and Czechia.

further reading

Christopher McIntosh's *The Swan King* tells the tale of Bavarian king Ludwig II, essential background for every visitor.

08

East Anglia,
ENGLAND

NORTH
SEA

Cley Marshes
Cromer
Holkham Hall

King's Lynn

• **Norwich**

• **Minsmere**

• **Cambridge**

Ipswich

Chelmsford

highlights

1 / Listen as the wind amongst the reeds creates a soul-soothing soundtrack at birding hotspots such as **Minsmere** and **Cley Marshes**.

2 / University-hop in **Cambridge**, visiting legendary libraries, exceptional museums and college greens that hosted Newton, Hawking, Darwin and the Monty Pythons.

3 / Have a night out in **Norwich**, Norfolk's cultured capital, enjoying theatre, live music, art shows and creative dining.

4 / Explore **North Norfolk** on local buses between Cromer and Kings Lynn, stopping for bird reserves, beaches, handsome **Holkham Hall** and East Anglia's best seafood.

E ngland's enigmatic east is a sampling platter of old England, without the usual touristy trinkets. Bundled together as East Anglia, the counties of Suffolk, Norfolk, Essex and Cambridgeshire are dotted with villages of half-timbered 16th-century houses and unexpectedly arty wool towns, backing a coastline studded with beaches and bird reserves that echo with the boom of bitterns every spring. Sure, there are popular spots (Cambridge; the Norfolk Broads waterways) but also timeless escapes, where participating in the 21st century feels entirely optional. After visiting, you won't see England in quite the same way again.

OLDE ENGLAND –
BUT THE REAL DEAL

After the trials and tribulations of the early 2020s, many travellers are desperate to escape the modern age, and East Anglia is happy to help out. The past seeps from the landscape in the former heartland of England's wool trade, where medieval money built palatial mansions, sky-piercing cathedrals and some of the world's most prestigious seats of learning. But this isn't the pre-packaged 'Ye Olde English Village' experience – history is a living thing out east. Traditional arts and crafts are fiercely protected and ancient architecture is lived in and preserved. Rent a cottage to stay in and it will probably come half-timbered, wonky and older than most modern nations.

Why visit in 2025? Because word is creeping out, and competition is growing for those dreamy, centuries-old cottages. Using the cities of Cambridge and Norwich as springboards to reach the Suffolk and Norfolk coastline, you'll feel the pace of life ease tangibly as you step off the train – an increasingly rare experience in this crowded island.

A FEAST FROM THE EAST

East Anglia was doing organic, local and seasonal long before it became cool. Meals here come layered and lavish – such as the inspired creations of Daniel Clifford at Cambridge's Midsummer House – or the agreeably unpretentious, like munching fish fresh off the boats and crisp chips in the charming coastal towns of Aldeburgh and Southwold. What you'll notice every-where are dishes leaning towards the sea. Thanks to the protected fisheries of the Wash, East Anglia never lost its taste for seafood, as other regions did when British fishing declined during WWII. Menus are

Norwich, cleaved by the River Wensum and topped by its magnificent cathedral **1** Looking down Cambridge's Trinity St to the tower of St John's College **2** Half-timbered heaven in the Suffolk village of Lavenham

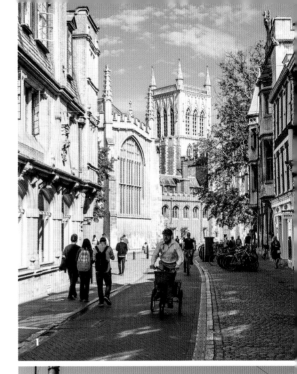

I love the quirky market towns with unusual shops and a real community vibe. There are also spectacular places to explore nature, such as Minsmere and Dersingham Bog, and some absolutely stunning scenery.

ANNETTE SALKALD
/ North Suffolk Coast Reserves warden,
  Royal Society for the Protection of Birds

alive with oysters and mussels, dressed crab, smoked fish, potted shrimp and more – even chip shops are getting in on the action, with lobster and chips and *moules marinières* popping up amongst the usual favourites. Foodies make a beeline for Cambridge, the Suffolk village of Dedham, the north Norfolk coast (where every village has its own seafood treat) and Norwich, where weekend dining options along St Benedicts St give London a run for its money.

EASTERN EDGE

Just because this region drips with history, don't imagine that it's stuck in the past. The east has a long history filled with orthodoxy-busting creativity, anti-establishmentarianism and rebellion – this is, after all, the home turf of king-killer Oliver Cromwell, pioneering music producer Brian Eno and warrior queen Boudicca. Small theatres, community arts centres and venues in converted churches showcase everything from radical political shows to performance art and thrash metal, particularly in student-oriented Norwich and Cambridge, where every second building seems to host something arty and

3 © Magdanatka Shutterstock 4 © Mark Caunt Shutterstock 5 © Archer Photo Shutterstock

5

unexpected. Music, both mainstream and eccentric, gets its dues at enthusiastic festivals such as Latitude and the Cambridge Folk Festival, and high culture gets a look in too, most famously at the Aldeburgh Festival, founded by former resident, composer Benjamin Britten. Then there's the visual arts scene, which buzzes with life at venues including Colchester's Firstsite, Houghton Hall's sculpture garden and Cambridge's Kettle's Yard. Pay attention to flyers and posters all over East Anglia – you never know what you'll stumble across.

3 Fruits of the sea for sale in Aldeburgh **4** Listen for the booming call of the elusive bittern at the RSPB's Minismere Nature Reserve **5** East Suffolk beachlife in Southwold

when to go

East Anglia is lovely in late summer, when long evenings demand trips to pub gardens and walks along the foreshore. From June to September, book ahead for accommodation, Broads boats and North Norfolk dining.

how to get there

There are fast and frequent train services to Cambridge, Norwich and Lowestoft. A hire car will make exploring easier, but local bus services connect most towns and villages.

further reading

Read Graham Swift's *Waterland* to be transported to the wartime Fens wetlands, or John Preston's *The Dig* for the backstory of the Sutton Hoo burial treasure.

09

Jordan Trail

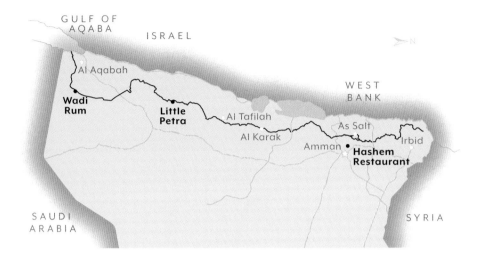

GULF OF
AQABA
ISRAEL
N
Al Aqabah
WEST
BANK
**Wadi
Rum**
**Little
Petra**
Al Tafilah
As Salt
Al Karak
Irbid
Amman • **Hashem
Restaurant**
SAUDI
ARABIA
SYRIA

ordan is something of a desert flower – a place of enduring peace and stability, blooming improbably in a troubled region. It's famed for lost cities from the ancient past, but it's also a fine place to take the pulse of the modern Middle East. And now there's another excellent reason to go – 2025 sees the Jordan Trail celebrating its tenth anniversary, making this the time to strike out on this dusty path through olive groves and silent *wadis* (river beds). There's no finer way to explore this fascinating country than on your own two feet.

NOT YOUR USUAL TRAIL

Fairly few people head to the Middle East to go hiking. Some are put off by the furnace-like temperatures. Others are daunted by lugging a backpack heavy with drinking

highlights

1 / Begin (or end) a Jordan Trail hike with a meal at **Hashem**, a legendary alfresco restaurant in the Jordanian capital, Amman – don't miss the falafel.

2 / Pass through the outpost of **Little Petra**, a Nabataean settlement around 8km (5 miles) north of Petra itself.

3 / Drink sugary cups of **mint tea** by the trailside – good fuel for the gruelling ascents of the Jordan Trail.

4 / Banish any vertigo and summon the courage to scale the sandstone rock arches of **Wadi Rum**.

water over parched miles. For many, this is a region synonymous with unpredictable borders, where roaming freely can seem impractical or even impossible. All this considered, the creation of the Jordan Trail in 2015 was a revolutionary act. Now celebrating its first decade, this 676km (420 miles) route stretches from the top to the bottom of Jordan – an epic journey during which walkers peel back layers of history and traverse miles of diverse and dazzling geography. Its northern trailhead lies in the orchards and olive groves along the Syrian border: its southernmost end sits where a red desert is lapped by the Red Sea. Walking even a small stretch reveals a side of the country most tourists miss entirely – for the Jordan Trail is, at its heart, a community enterprise. By day, hikers might be guided by local shepherds, stopping to sip tea boiled on a brushwood campfire. By night, tired walkers sleep on mattresses under the stars, in camps supported by local Bedouin. Jordan is a country defined by its hospitality, and this is a path along which you'll regularly encounter it.

HIKE HIGHLIGHTS

The Jordan Trail has been plotted so that it passes many of the nation's highlights. There's the scorching, saline expanse of the Dead Sea – the lowest dry point on the planet – and the Martian monoliths of Wadi Rum. As well as landscapes, you continually

The Martian-esque landscape of Wadi Rum **1** A scrap of shade beneath the Wadi Rum rocks **2** Camping out under the stars on the Jordan Trail hike

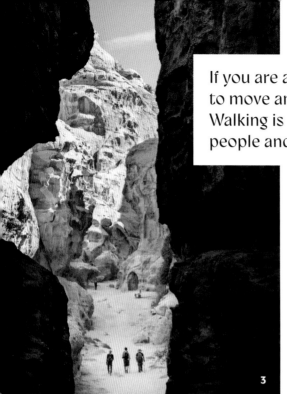

> If you are a Bedouin, having the freedom to move and go where you want is essential. Walking is my life – walk with the right people and you will always smile.

MOHAMMED AL HOMRAN
/ Shepherd and Jordan Trail guide

3

4

see the remnants of fallen civilisations by the trailside: the ancient Hellenistic city of Gadara is a prelude to the Crusades-era castle at Ajloun which, in turn, is rivalled by the hulking battlements of Karak Castle. For most, however, one ancient city eclipses all others: Petra. The four-day section of the Jordan Trail from Dana to Petra counts as the most popular and perhaps most beautiful leg. On it, walkers get a new perspective on the legendary rock-hewn city, sensing how ancient wayfarers would have crossed the *wadis* to enter into its sanctuary. This leg has plenty of other surprises too. You might hear the clattering hooves of Nubian ibex in the canyons of the Dana Biosphere Reserve. You might spend the night stargazing in Feynan Ecolodge, a beautiful off-grid, candle-lit hotel, whose roof terrace offers sublime views up to constellations. You will certainly find yourself far from civilisation in the remote expanse of Wadi Feid – a place of deep-gouged canyons – before jostling with crowds only a day or two later entering

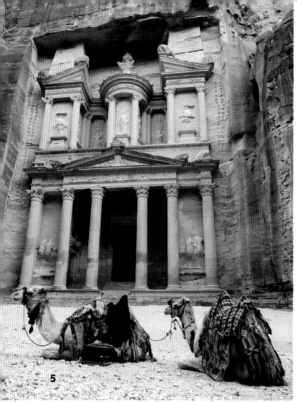

the city of Petra itself, watching the facade of the Monastery shimmer in the heat haze. Whether you stop in Petra to explore the murky tombs carved by the Nabataean people two millennia ago, or push on southward to Wadi Rum, you'll realise that the Jordan Trail ranks among the world's greatest long-distance paths. It is truly a national epic. The only catch is: you will definitely need to lug around a backpack full of drinking water.

3 Walking the steep *wadis* along the Jordan Trail route
4 Trailside sustenance in a Bedouin tent **5** Petra's Al-Khazneh, aka the Treasury **6** Taking in Petra from above

when to go

Jordan's tourism industry tends to get going in the shoulder season – from February to May and September to November. If you're planning on walking the Jordan Trail, it's wise to travel during this time to avoid the heat of high summer – you might also choose to travel in winter (though be aware there is occasional snow on high ground, such as the escarpment around Dana). Look out for guided through-hikes on the Jordan Trail website, hosted around twice a year.

how to get there

Almost all visitors to Jordan transit through Queen Alia International Airport in the capital, Amman, which has a broad range of international flights. Jordan's efficient JETT bus network connects to hubs along the Jordan Trail – including Petra and Wadi Rum.

10

Mt Hood & THE
COLUMBIA RIVER GORGE, USA

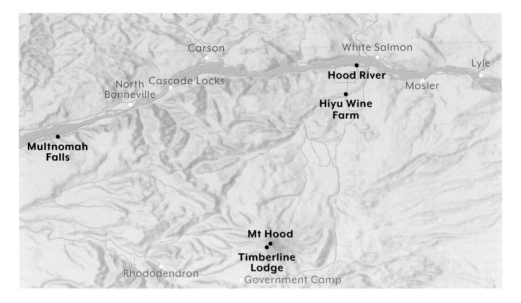

Does your perfect travel day involve an 8km (5 miles) hike to a waterfall, or are you more of a glass of wine on the balcony overlooking a vineyard kind of person? Visit the Mt Hood region and there's no need to choose: you can have both. Just 40 minutes outside of food-focused Portland, one of the Pacific Northwest's most distinctive geographic areas has nurtured a laid-back community where inventive, sustainable cuisine is becoming as big a draw as the outdoor adventures Mt Hood is already known for.

GET OUT THERE

Few landscapes are this densely packed with diverse terrain but also accessible and rewarding for the adventure-seeker. Skiers, snowboarders, hikers and windsurfers have been in on the secret for decades. Where else can you start an epic 64km (40 miles) round-the-mountain hike like the Timberline Trail from literally the parking lot of a historic luxury

highlights

1 / Seek out **Hiyu Wine Farm**, a vineyard-and-restaurant offering natural wines made using the 'field blends' technique, in which different varietals are planted and co-fermented together.

2 / Hike **Multnomah Falls**, where the views are stunning year-round and trails lead visitors to several other waterfalls.

3 / Stay in luxury at 'parkitecture' gem **Timberline Lodge** atop Mt Hood. The breakfast here is legendary.

4 / Try windsurfing in the fun, outdoorsy town of **Hood River**, known as the windsurfing capital of the world, and with great food and beer too.

hotel? Or wrap up a kayaking session with a craft brew and burger waiting just steps away? People who come here for outdoor recreation are starting to catch on that it's also an amazing place to eat and drink.

From the densely forested slopes of the Columbia River Gorge to the craggy peak of Mt Hood and the orchards and berry patches in between, there's an impressive amount of variety crammed into a compact area here. One result is the huge number of microclimates, which is excellent for growing apples, pears, berries – and grapes. The gorge is coming into its own as a serious wine region, after some early years in the shadow of the more famous Willamette Valley. The key? All that variety. Those different microclimates mean many different varietals of wine grapes thrive here. And anywhere there's good wine, there's always good food.

THE FRUIT LOOP

The Hood River Valley is home to around 30 different farm stands, orchards, wineries, cideries and brewers who excel at producing the ultimate expression of the valley's agricultural bounty, whether in the field, in the glass or on the plate. Apple, pear and cherry trees have been cultivated here since the 1850s, with brewpubs, cideries and farm-to-table dining coming along more recently. The Fruit Loop, a 56km (35 miles) scenic drive on country roads, lets you pick and choose the best.

Golden hour in the Columbia River Gorge **1** Ramona Falls, on the west side of Mt Hood **2** Apple orchard in blossom in the Hood River Valley

Hug a giant evergreen, sit by a crisp river, stop to admire a tiny mushroom emerging from a stump. Whatever path you choose, be prepared for the sensational feeling of awe.

AMANDA PARROTT
/ Hood River resident

Wander through a multi-generational family farm like Draper Girls or Kiyokawa Family Orchards in the hamlet of Parkdale and hand-pick your own produce. Or grab a jar of blackberry jam or a pint of unfiltered cider and enjoy the local fruit in its final form. Duck into a tasting room at one of several local wineries and pick up a bottle of whatever takes your fancy. Within a few miles you'll have the makings of a locally sourced feast to fortify you before hitting the slopes or trails.

SAVOURING TRADITION

Salmon and steelhead have long travelled the Columbia River to spawn, and are among the most important food sources in the Pacific Northwest; Indigenous people from the Yakama, Warm Springs, Umatilla and Nez Perce have harvested these fish for thousands of years. Traditionally, fishers stand on wooden scaffolding and catch salmon with dip nets attached to long poles

– a tactic that requires strength and skill. Today, visitors can buy fish caught this way as well as by more modern methods, directly from the fishers, right on the river bank – good luck finding fresher salmon than that. Look for 'Fresh Fish' signs near the Bridge of the Gods, or try the Brigham Fish Market in Cascade Locks, run by two sisters who belong to the Confederated Tribes of the Umatilla Indian Reservation.

when to go

Spring (April-May) and fall (September-October) offer the best combination of fair weather, wildflowers and fresh produce. The mid-July and August heat can be wilting, but it's also peach season. Winter brings skiers and snowboarders to Mt Hood.

how to get there

Portland International Airport is less than 96km (60 miles) from Hood River.

further reading

Martin Marten by Brian Doyle is a joy-filled novel about a boy living in a cabin on Mt Hood and a pine marten, both coming of age. For a biography of the mountain itself, read *On Mt Hood* by Jon Bell.

3 A snowcapped Mt Hood from Washington side of Columbia River Gorge **4** Charcuterie plate at an Oregon winery tasting session **5** The Multnomah Falls hike is a Columbia River Gorge highlight **6** The snaking and scenic Historic Columbia River Hwy

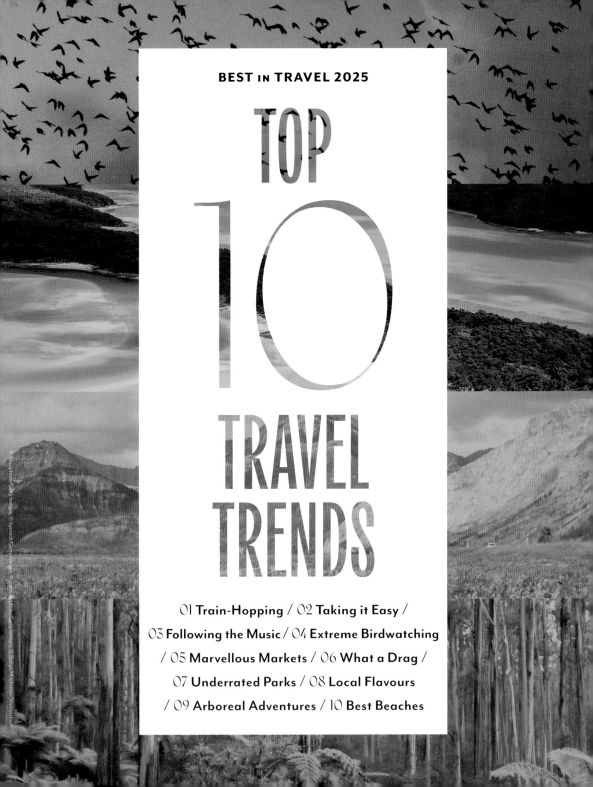

BEST IN TRAVEL 2025

TOP 10 TRAVEL TRENDS

01 Train-Hopping / 02 Taking it Easy /
03 Following the Music / 04 Extreme Birdwatching
/ 05 Marvellous Markets / 06 What a Drag /
07 Underrated Parks / 08 Local Flavours
/ 09 Arboreal Adventures / 10 Best Beaches

TRAIN-HOPPING

THE TOP 10 BEST TRAIN TRIPS

From cross-continental epics to slow travel branch lines, these rail-based adventures make the journey an experience in itself.

01 / Shonan Monorail, Japan

This short but mighty *danglebahn* (a train suspended from the rail above it) offers a thrilling 6.5km (4 miles) route for Tokyo and Yokohama residents (and visitors) heading for the beaches, baths and parks around Enoshima. If Japan's too far for a dangle, try Shonan's twin sister in Wuppertal, Germany.

02 / The Skeena (Prince Rupert to Jasper), Canada

In a country of stunning rail journeys, this is the tip of the moose's antler. An unbeatably scenic two-day adventure through the Rockies, with a Prince George stopover to maximise daylight sightseeing.

03 / The Sunset Limited, USA

A true American epic, The Sunset Limited makes a thrice-weekly pilgrimage from New Orleans to Los Angeles via San Antonio, Tucson and Phoenix. It crosses five states in 48 hours, brushes the Mexican border and, once beyond the Southwest and into California, its terminus is just a taxi ride from the Pacific.

04 / Septemvri–Dobrinishte, Bulgaria

Amble off the main line between Sofia and Plovdiv to tackle this venerable narrow-gauge route: part tourist service, part local lifeline. Expect spiralling ascents and dizzying views climbing up as high as Avramovo – at 1267m (4157ft) it's the highest station in the Balkans.

05 / Cuba's changing railways

New rolling stock has sped up services and improved reliability, comfort and facilities on the main Havana–Santiago de Cuba line. On other stretches, including the iconic Hershey Line, the unpredictably old-school experience is all part of the fun.

06 / Bentham Line, England

This near-secret railway runs from Leeds in Yorkshire, to Morecambe, on the Lancashire coast. Enjoy the Bentham Line a scenic day out in itself, or use it as a gateway to cosy pub stays and walks in the Yorkshire Dales National Park from Clapham and Giggleswick stations.

07 / Montpellier–Perpignan, France

Fast TGVs (high-speed trains) from Paris to the south of France unfussily slow down and hug the coastline, particularly while passing Béziers and Narbonne. Sit on the left if heading 'down' France for Mediterranean views and to spot flamboyances of flamingos in the seaside saline waters.

4

08 / The Karwar Express, India

After sampling the craft beer and coffee-fuelled delights of Bengaluru (Bangalore), a trip on the Karwar Express is the perfect preparation for some languid downtempo beach life in Gokarna. It takes just over 15 hours to travel through and enjoy 711km (450 miles) of tropical greenery, in particular the section of rolling hills between Sakleshpura and Subramanya.

09 / Le Train du Desert Iron Ore train, Mauritania

Arguably travel's filthiest frontier, to ride on the Train du Desert through the Mauritanian Sahara, from Zouérat to Nouadhibou, is to endure a day and a night in the open, travelling on a pile of freshly mined mineral dust. There is a seated car, but that's not really the point. Seek and heed local advice.

10 / Brașov–Ploiești, Romania

This scenic section of the longer train journey from Budapest to Bucharest travels through evocative Carpathian forests, home to bears, hiking trails and castles. The area contains Romania's best-known ski resorts too – which is where, in winter, most of your fellow passengers will be headed.

TAKING IT EASY

THE TOP 10 PLACES TO JUST RELAX

Slow travel may sound like marketing, but for many of us it's a way of life, bringing us closer to nature and clearing our minds of the gunk of modern life.

01 / Lough Erne, Northern Ireland

Two freshwater lakes, linked by a river, comprise Lough Erne, a mesmerising blend of snaking waterways and hidden bays. Once home to monasteries that were leading centres of learning and innovation, the lough's islands are now occupied mostly by birds and livestock.

02 / Indian Pacific Rail Journey, Australia

Connecting Adelaide and Perth, the highlight of this two-night train trip is a day devoted to the desert, particularly the fascinating Nullarbor Plain with its complete absence of trees. Enjoy a cocktail while gazing out the window as nothingness slides past.

03 / Nagaland, India

You can spend weeks in Nagaland without seeing a single fellow visitor. Long considered the 'wild east' Nagaland abounds in primeval beauty and tribal culture. Its dazzling hills and valleys. are otherworldly places.

04 / Tubagua, Dominican Republic

Radically different from the popular coastal resorts in the DR, inland Tubagua is a perfect place to absorb the nuances of authentic Dominican life through community tourism projects. It's also home to one of the Caribbean's best eco-lodges, Tubagua Ecolodge.

05 / Big Bend National Park, USA

The mountains meet the desert in Big Bend, a vast national park tucked into a remote corner of west Texas. This place receives fewer than 10% of the Grand Canyon's visitors, which means that adventures and multi-day excursions – like rafting on the Rio Grande – are easier to book.

06 / Ibo Island, Mozambique

A crossroads of cultures with a tempestuous history, this island in Mozambique's Quirimbas archipelago is so off-the-grid that you need to charter a plane to get there. Dilapidated villas and crumbling, moss-covered buildings line its car-free streets. The Quirimbas National Park contains most of the southern Quirimbas islands (including Ibo, Medjumbe and Matemo) along with a large tract of coastal mangrove and forest on the mainland. Visit gorgeous beaches and scattered coral islands, and stay at an ecofriendly resort.

07 / Jökulsárlón, Iceland

Witness icebergs calving from Europe's largest glacier, Fjallsjökull. They drift towards the sea and, almost there, strand themselves on the sandbanks of the massive Jökulsárlón lagoon, which was once entirely glacier.

08 / Tatai River, Cambodia

Winding through a remote jungle that's home to all manner of birds and wildlife, a journey here is a uniquely tranquil experience, with almost all access by boat or kayak and nights spent listening to the sounds of the rainforest.

09 / Bwindi, Uganda

Sharing time with mountain gorillas in the wilds of Uganda's rainforests is utterly magical. Nothing prepares you for their sheer beauty and brawn, their soulful brown eyes, their astonishingly human-like expressions and their extraordinarily gentle demeanour.

10 / Atacama Desert, Chile

Unfurling across northern Chile in sizzling salt flats, bone-dry sierras, barren beaches and prickly patches of colourful cacti, the Atacama's incredibly clear night sky is probably its greatest attribute. Stargazing from Earth's most lunar-like landscape is truly a life-changer.

FOLLOWING THE MUSIC ♪♫

THE TOP 10 BEST VENUES

A music venue is almost as important as, well, the music. These 10 stand-out temples of sound are worth a trip on their own.

01 / The Ryman, Nashville, USA

The Ryman Auditorium is Nashville's premier music venue. This historic stage was the original home of the Grand Ole Opry and where superstars like Dolly Parton, Hank Williams and Johnny Cash jump-started their careers.

02 / Hayden Homes Amphitheater, Bend, USA

A summer concert in Bend's biggest backyard is a music lover's dream. Located along Oregon's Deschutes River, this intimate yet expansive spot has plenty of chill. Bring a chair, grab a local brew, graze the food trucks and let the music move you.

03 / Rudolfinum, Prague, Czech Republic

The grand Rudolfinum, designed in 1884 by architects Josef Schulz and Josef Zítek, is considered one of Prague's finest neo-Renaissance buildings. It's home to the Czech Philharmonic Orchestra and the impressive Dvořák Hall, one of the Czech capital's great venues for classical music.

04 / De Barra's Folk Club, Cork, Ireland

Known as the 'Carnegie Hall of Cork' – with walls splattered with photos and press cuttings, dramatic masks and musical instruments – this Clonakilty stalwart is one of Ireland's top spots to listen to traditional Irish folk music, with a perfectly poured pint in your hand.

05 / Dalhalla Amphitheatre, Rattvik, Sweden

Dug into the limestone bedrock of a former quarry in the middle of the forest near Rättvik, this sunken, open-air venue benefits from incredible acoustics. Its stunning setting is as much of a draw as the various rock and opera performances that take place during the summer.

06 / Hollywood Bowl, Los Angeles, USA

Summers in LA wouldn't be the same without alfresco melodies under the stars at the Bowl, a huge natural stadium in the Hollywood Hills. Its annual season – which usually runs from June to September – includes symphonies, jazz bands and iconic acts.

07 / Royal Opera House, Mumbai, India

Commissioned by King George V and originally completed in 1916, India's only surviving opera house reopened to suitably dramatic fanfare exactly a century later after being shuttered in the 1990s. Portraits of musicians are painted on the ceiling of this Chowpatty-area landmark.

08 / Melbourne Forum, Melbourne, Australia

One of the city's most atmospheric live-music venues, the Forum's striking Moorish exterior (an over-the-top fantasia of minarets, domes and dragons) houses an equally interesting interior, with the southern hemisphere's night sky rendered on the domed ceiling.

09 / Municipal Theatre, Ho Chi Minh City, Vietnam

Built in 1898 and also known as the Saigon Opera House, this theatre is one of the city's most recognisable buildings. The only way to get inside and see its elegant chandeliers, bronze statues and pretty granite floors is to attend a performance.

10 / Mansa Floating Hub, Mindelo, Cape Verde

Designed to resist the effects of climate change, this 'floating music hub' consists of three sustainable timber, connected A-frame structures. Designed by Kunlé Adeyemi of Amsterdam-based firm NLÉ, the venue hosts a rotating slate of performers.

EXTREME BIRDWATCHING

THE TOP 10 AVIAN SPECIES TO LOOK OUT FOR

It takes a bad-ass bird to thrive in some of the world's most extraordinary environments. Discover 10 of our most remarkable feathered friends and the places they call home.

01 / Cassowary, Australia

If birds were bands, the cassowary would be Black Sabbath. Up to 2m (6ft) tall, clad in shaggy, black plumage and sporting a heavy-duty helmet, this beast patrols Queensland's Daintree Rainforest.

07 / **Starling, Italy**

Swirling over Rome's skyline, flocks of starlings ebb and flow in a shape-shifting display at dusk in the Eternal City. The best months for witnessing a murmuration are December and January.

08 / **Great horned owl, USA**

If looks could kill, the great horned owl would be America's deadliest avian predator. Their range covers most of the USA, ruling wild places such as Yellowstone National Park.

09 / **Takahē, New Zealand**

Thought extinct until rediscovered in the South Island's Fiordland in 1948, the rotund takahē is the largest of New Zealand's flightless birds. Just 500 survive, but several chicks hatched in 2023.

10 / **Capercaillie, Scotland**

That glugging sound you might hear in a Scottish pine forest could be a courting capercaillie, the stoutest of the grouse. Start your capercaillie quest in the Cairngorms National Park.

02 / **Puffin, Iceland**

Puffins may have a comical demeanour but their daily life is no joke. Setting out to sea, they fly up to 50km (31 miles) to collect fish for their families.

03 / **Andean condor, Peru**

Peru's Colca Canyon is almost twice as deep as the USA's Grand Canyon. On its thermals soar Andean condors with their 3m (10ft) wingspans. Slow to reproduce, only 7000 remain.

04 / **Red-crowned crane, Japan**

In late winter, on Hokkaidō's snowy stage, pairs of red-crowned cranes perform mesmerising courtship dances. With synchronised steps and twirls, these elegant birds reaffirm lifelong commitments to each other.

05 / **Peregrine falcon, England**

Described by JA Baker in *The Peregrine* (1967) as falling 'like a heart in flames' upon its prey, today the world's fastest falcons spy their next meals from London's high-rises.

06 / **Golden Eagle, Mongolia**

Trained golden eagles grip the forearms of traditional Kazakh hunters on horseback in western Mongolia as bird and human survey the Altai Mountains.

MARVELLOUS MARKETS

THE TOP 10 BEST MARKETS

Shopping at a local market is a satisfying way to get to know a place and its people. Wake up early (and check the calendar) and experience first-hand local customs, delicacies and wares.

01 / Tha Kha Floating Market, Bangkok, Thailand

Tha Kha may not be the most famous, but it is a local favourite, known for home-made cooking, sellers showcasing produce grown in their own gardens and the requisite rowboats. Arrive early in the morning or visit at night when the fireflies come out and light up the trees.

02 / Marché Atwater, Montréal, Canada

Housed in a 1933 brick hall off the Canal de Lachine, this market has it all: fresh produce from local farms, excellent wines, crusty bread and more, best devoured picnic-style on the grassy banks near the water.

03 / Pike Place, Seattle, USA

You haven't lived until you've witnessed the fish fly at this Seattle hotspot. If taking a whole salmon home isn't an option, pick up treats from any of its speciality food stores, offering everything from momos (Nepalese dumplings) to doughnuts.

04 / Queens Night Market, New York City, USA

The scene at this seasonal night market is an olfactory bonanza, befitting an NYC venue that celebrates innovation. Here, young up-and-coming cooks ply their trade, turning out a plethora of cuisines and infusions at a mercifully low price point.

05 / Marché des Lices, Rennes, France

Every Saturday, France's second-largest market comes alive. For 400 years, shoppers have been procuring Brittany's best fish, meat, produce, cheese and much more from an array of indoor and outdoor stalls and food trucks.

06 / Neighbourgoods Market, Cape Town, South Africa

On weekends, locals and visitors congregate to see and taste the region's freshest produce, oysters, wine and coffee, along with global dishes made with locally sourced ingredients. Communal tables up the feeling of camaraderie.

07 / Nishiki-kōji Ichiba, Kyoto, Japan

Nishiki Market is a wonder for anyone with a passion for cooking and eating. Known locally as 'Kyoto's kitchen', high-end restaurateurs shop for ingredients here, while visitors can ogle the unusual foods that go into the city's traditional cuisine.

08 / Farm Gate Market, Hobart/Nipaluna, Tasmania

When Sunday morning rolls around, Farm Gate (aka Farmy) comes alive with local purveyors hawking their bounty of locally produced items: fruit and veg, baked goods, spirits. Before perusing, fill your belly with breakfast from the food trucks at Farmy's Grub Hub.

09 / Mercado San Pedro, Cuzco, Peru

The food on offer at vibrant San Pedro Market – designed by Gustave Eiffel, of 'tower' fame – runs the gamut from fresh fruit and smoothies to fall-off-the-bone beef ribs and river fish. This place is a feast for the senses – though the aromas are the most alluring.

10 / Khari Baoli, Old Delhi, India

This famous labyrinth of spice and colour feels frozen in time. There's a throat-tickling pungency hanging in the air and mountains of lentils and rice, enormous jars of chutneys, nuts and teas at every turn. Your clothes will smell delicious for days.

WHAT A DRAG

THE TOP 10 MOST SPECTACULAR DRAG SHOWS

Drag is more than RuPaul and her queen coven – it's a global art form featuring boundary-breakers who defy cultural norms by holding up a mirror to society. Take a look.

01 / Paris, France

Edith Piaf rises from the dead to perform alongside Lady Gaga and Celine Dion impersonators at Chez Michou, a Montmartre cabaret for *transformiste* drag artists, belting ballads since 1956.

02 / **Provincetown, USA**

Every summer, old-school drag artists bring bawdy cabarets to Provincetown, the queer-friendly tip of Cape Cod's curling peninsula. Don't miss bedraggled chanteuse Dina Martina, beloved for wacky warbling.

03 / **Berlin, Germany**

Non-conformist kings, queens and performers-in-between rule Berlin's uber-queer nightlife scene. Watch them compete at November's Mx. Kotti competition, a transgressive take on beauty pageantry.

04 / **London, England**

High-octane drag performances paint plenty of London's nightlife venues pink, but things get particularly colourful for summer's Lipsync1000, when up-and-comers show off their oral skills at the Clapham Grand finale.

05 / **Bangkok, Thailand**

What to expect at House of Heals, owned by *Drag Race Thailand* co-host Pangina? Tight tucks, faultless mugs and performances six nights a week atop the Renaissance Hotel.

06 / **New York City, USA**

NYC goes on a two-day gender bender for Bushwig – a September drag fest that skews more 'punk rock princess' than 'bedazzled prom queen', with non-stop performances in an industrial warehouse.

5

07 / **Sydney, Australia**

In late February, Australia's drag darlings reign supreme on the western side of Darlinghurst's Oxford St – an LGTBIQ+ epicentre with non-stop entertainment during Sydney Gay & Lesbian Mardi Gras.

08 / **Puerto Vallarta, Mexico**

Winter in North America is a drag – unless you're in tropical 'PV', Mexico's LGBTIQ+ riviera, where gown clowns at the Palm Cabaret impersonate divas and improvise with crowds.

09 / **Chicago, USA**

To win the Miss Continental crown during Chicago's cut-throat Labour Day pageant is to enter the pantheon of high-heel royalty, worth international praise.

10 / **Barcelona, Spain**

Hop around Barcelona's best LGBTIQ+ bars and allied establishments on the Ravalda Drag Tour, spotlighting a kaleidoscope of Catalonian gender magicians, often hosted bi-monthly.

UNDERRATED PARKS

THE TOP 10 MOST UNDERRATED NATIONAL PARKS

The most popular national parks can mean long lines, crowds and high prices.
But there are thousands of others around the world, much less visited but equally
deserving of their NP status, and all offering beauty, splendour and wonder.

01 / Canyonlands National Park, Utah, USA

Hiking takes on a new meaning in Canyonlands when you're scrambling up and down cliffs. Trek the Slickrock Trail for 360-degree views and incredible rock formations.

02 / Voyageurs National Park, Minnesota, USA

Some 40% of Voyageurs is fresh water, making it a wetland wonderland where you can canoe, camp, repeat to your heart's content. There's zero light pollution too so the sky at night is dazzling.

03 / Waterton Lakes National Park, Alberta, Canada

Waterton Lakes' appeal lies in its rugged high alpine environments swathed in wildflowers. Take the Red Rock Canyon hike to see two rushing waterfalls, then recharge with scones and tea at the Prince of Wales hotel.

04 / Nuuksio National Park, Espoo, Finland

Immerse yourself in Finnish nature and spot wildlife on a day trip from Helsinki to Nuuksio. Go in the winter when you can cross-country ski through wooded Ice-Age-chiselled valleys.

05 / Bannau Brycheiniog/ Brecon Beacons National Park, Powys, Wales

Simultaneously bleak and beautiful, Brecon Beacons is ideal for an atmospheric wander. Walk the 159km (99 miles), eight-day Beacons Way Trail and you'll see all the park's highest summits and beautiful moors.

06 / Parque Nacional De Ordesa y Monte Perdido, Huesca, Spain

Ordesa y Monte Perdido is Pyrenees high country at its most spectacular. The hikes here are challenging, so choose the Faja de Pelay route, which has the added benefit of being the most breathtaking.

07 / Cockscomb Basin Wildlife Sanctuary, Stann Creek District, Belize

A protected park in Belize where jaguars roam free. Maybe you'll spot one if you stay the night, listening to the jungle noises as you take a guided after-dark hike.

08 / Ranthambore National Park, Rajasthan, India

The best place to spot wild tigers in Rajasthan, Ranthambore also features crocodile-filled lakes and ancient temples. Book two or three safaris into the jungle to give you ample opportunity to see a tiger.

09 / Tsavo West National Park, Coast Province, Kenya

Covering a huge variety of landscapes, from swamps to volcanic cones, Tsavo is true African wilderness. Make your way to Rhino Valley for lions, elephants, giraffes and possibly a black rhino.

10 / Great Sandy National Park, Queensland, Australia

Possibilities for adventure are dizzying in Great Sandy – and most of them involve its namesake feature. Take a 4WD through stunning scenery along the beach from Noosa North Shore to Double Island Point.

LOCAL FLAVOURS

THE TOP 10 BEST FOOD EXPERIENCES

Eating and travel are inextricably linked, no matter what your tastes. These destinations are worth the trip for their distinctive and delicious local flavours.

01 / Bibimbap, South Korea

This Korean culinary staple of rice with a crusty bottom is served in a hot stone pot layered with veggies, egg and occasionally meat. Top it off with red *gochujang* (chilli paste) and give it a stir to best savour the layered flavours and textures.

02 / Cozido das Furnas, the Azores, Portugal

You'll find this singular stew only in the Furnas region of São Miguel in the Azores archipelago. It cooks in fumaroles underground for five to seven hours, its vegetables and meat infused with a smoky touch of sulphur from the warm volcanic soil.

03 / Jerk, Jamaica

Jamaica's spicy jerk marinade is doused on meats and fish, then smoked slowly outdoors over a pimento-wood fire. Scotch bonnet chillies bring the heat, and allspice rounds out the piquant flavour – always order the jerk!

04 / Asado, Argentina

Argentina is known for the quality and preparation of its beef: salting the meat then slow cooking it on a grill with slanted runners that funnel the fat to the sides, while an adjustable height system directs the perfect amount of heat to the meat.

05 / Jollof rice, West Africa

The origins of this vibrant, celebratory dish are the subject of some debate: a 'joloff-off', so to speak, among West African nations. But whether you sample jollof in Nigeria or Senegal, Gambia or Ghana, expect to find similar foundational ingredients: tomatoes, peppers, onions and herbs.

06 / Pho, Vietnam

Ubiquitous throughout the country, this comforting noodle soup is inextricably linked with Vietnamese culture. Slurp as much as you can, as often as you can, be it on a street corner in Hanoi or at Michelin-starred Anan Saigon in Ho Chi Minh City.

07 / Biriyani, India

Hyderabad is commonly thought to be the epicentre of biryani, the flavourful rice-based dish one might find at Indian restaurants the world over. However, the variations found in other parts of the country, from the more vegetable-forward Assamese biryanis to Kerala's prawn, beef and fish varieties, showcase subtler, more complex flavours than their well-known counterparts.

6

08 / Hoppers, Sri Lanka

Made with a fermented batter of rice flour and coco-nut milk, *hoppers* – also known as *appa* or *appam* – are bowl-shaped pancakes with crispy edges and fluffy middles. Plain *hoppers* usually come with the chilli-and-salt condiment *lunu miris*.

09 / Momos, Nepal

Wander the streets of capital Kathmandu, or any town in Nepal, and you'll see these delicious dump-lings everywhere; steamed or fried and filled with sweet or savoury ingredients – apples, chocolate, vegetables, fish, water buffalo.

10 / Lamingtons, Australia

While Australia and New Zealand like to duke it out over ownership of the pavlova (the meringue and fruit dessert), Australia is indisputably the home of the lamington: a sponge cake coated in chocolate before being rolled in coconut might sound simple, but it's unbelievably good.

ARBOREAL ADVENTURES

THE TOP 10 BEST TREE TOURISM DESTINATIONS

Tall and silent or fragrant with blossom? Whatever your type, spend time with your dream tree in these 10 places around the world and reconnect with nature.

01 / Gingko, China

Seeds of the *Gingko biloba* were being prescribed in Chinese medicine thousands of years ago, and are still used today. See a golden gingko, planted during the Tang dynasty, in Xi'an.

02 / Mountain ash, Australia

Ribbons of bark peel off lofty mountain ash trees, raucous cockatoo calls fill the air and the understorey explodes with giant ferns – this is Victoria's Yarra Ranges National Park.

03 / Kauri, New Zealand

Growing only on the northwest tip of New Zealand's North Island, hefty kauri trees play a crucial role in Maōri creation stories. Enjoy an audience with the kings of Waipoua Forest.

04 / Oak, England

Robin Hood hid among them: King Charles II hid up one in 1651; and they lend their name to 400 British pubs. Meet an English oak in Nottinghamshire's Sherwood Forest.

05 / Olive, Greece

Some of Greece's olive trees have been growing since the time of Alexander the Great, more than 2300 years ago. The oldest and gnarliest can be found in villages on Crete.

06 / Coast redwood, USA

Breathe deeply and feel time slow in the calming presence of northern California's coastal redwoods. These giants are protected in the group of Redwood National and State Parks.

07 / Almond, Spain

Almond trees thrive in the foothills of the Tramuntana Mountains on Mallorca, and from January through February, the island's orchards are a blizzard of white petals as the fruit trees blossom.

08 / Cherry, Japan

Sakura, the blossom of Japan's celebrated cherry trees, sweeps south to north from March. The pink blooms spark *hanami*, flower-viewing outings. Bring a picnic to appreciate the flowers with friends.

09 / Baobab, Madagascar

The more bulbous a baobab's trunk, the more water it is storing – which is why elephants tear into them. Visit the trees (minus elephants) on Madagascar's Avenue of the Baobabs.

10 / Lebanon cedar, Lebanon

This biblical symbol of strength was once highly sought-after for woodworking and shipbuilding. Today, Lebanon's Forest of the Cedars of God, in the Qadisha Valley, has UNESCO World Heritage Status.

BEST BEACHES

THE TOP 10 BEST BEACHES

It's nearly impossible to whittle a list of top beaches down to 10, but we did our best. These are the shining stars – the most magical, don't-miss-out, popular-for-a-reason stretches of sand from around the globe.

01 / Whitehaven Beach, Queensland, Australia

The swirling pattern of aquamarine water and snow-white sandbars at the northern end of Whitehaven Beach is otherworldly – and the average water temperature is 26°C (79°F) year-round, so there's no excuse for not getting wet.

02 / Squeaky Beach, Victoria, Australia

A standout in Wilsons Promontory, this protected slice of wilderness is fringed by Victoria's largest marine national park. The quartz sand compresses under your feet, creating a high-pitched squeak, and if you get tired of that you can splash in hidden rock pools or dive into the crystalline ocean.

03 / Anse Source d'Argent, La Digue, Seychelles

This place lives up to the hype. Its dazzling white sands are lapped by shallow turquoise waters and backed by beautiful granite boulders spilling onto the beach like a work of art. It's heaven on Earth.

04 / Sunset Beach, Trang, Thailand

The prettiest beach among the jaunty rock forma-tions, emerald waters and jungle-shrouded hills in the Trang Islands of Thailand's far southern Andaman Coast. It's a worthwhile short hike or longtail boat ride to watch the namesake sunset.

05 / Sarakiniko Beach, Milos, Greece

There's no sand at Sarakiniko. Instead you find a surreal volcanic landscape that folds into the deep, blue-green Aegean, and stone arches, alabaster cliffs, disused mining tunnels and dimly lit caves that create a mesmerising contrast with the endless sea.

06 / Haukland Beach, Lofoten Islands, Norway

Watching the northern lights reflecting off snow-white sands feels like pure magic. Haukland is one of the most unbelievably beautiful beaches among Norway's thousands, and in summer the midnight sun bathes the whole place in an eerie glow.

07 / Playa Balandra, Baja California Sur, Mexico

The stunning Playa Balandra is an enclosed cove with shallow turquoise water perfect for kids. Rent kayaks or stand-up paddleboards, explore tidepools, hike to neighbouring coves and gaze at the surreal rock for-mations of Espíritu Santo across the sparkling water.

08 / Pfeiffer Beach, California, USA

In late December, the setting sun illuminates Pfeiffer's Keyhole Arch and a sliver of coast with a golden light – an unparalleled work of nature along the Big Sur shoreline. And after rainstorms, the beach can turn purple from manganese garnet in the crumbling bluffs.

09 / Hanalei Bay, Hawai'i , USA

The last place on Earth or a doorstep to the heavens? The difference hardly matters when admiring Kaua'i's Hanalei Bay, a 3.2km (2 miles) crescent of golden sand carved from the northern edge of the northernmost island in the Hawaiian archipelago.

10 / Platja Illetes, Formentera, Spain

From the clear Caribbean-blue waters to the carefree Mediterranean-island vibe, there's nowhere quite like barefoot, salty-aired Formentera, where Platja Illetes evokes all that's magical about this beach paradise.

Best in Travel 2025

October 2024

Published by Lonely Planet Global Limited

CRN 554153

www.lonelyplanet.com

1 2 3 4 5 6 7 8 9 10

Publishing Director Piers Pickard
Publisher Becca Hunt
Senior Editor Robin Barton
Editors Clifton Wilkinson, Polly Thomas
Designers Cat Grishaver, Emily Dubin
Cartographer Daniela Machova
Print Production Nigel Longuet

Andrew Bain (Launceston & The Tamar Valley), Joel Balsam (Slovakia), Jonny Bierman (Fiji), Margot Bigg (Puducherry), Joe Bindloss (East Anglia), Laurence Blair (Paraguay), Nitya Chambers (Pittsburgh), Tenille Clarke (Trinidad & Tobago), Virginia DiGaetano (Genoa), Marc Di Duca (Bavaria), Ismet Ersoy (Gireson & Ordu), Brekke Fletcher (Following the Music; Local Flavours; Marvellous Markets; Taking it Easy), John Garry (What a Drag), Lucie Grace (Osaka), Tom Hall (Introduction; Train-Hopping), Anthony Ham (Cameroon), Anita Isalska (Slovakia), Diego Jimeno (Chriqui), Shafik Meghji (The Terai), Isabella Noble (Palma), Becky Ohlsen (Mount Hood & the Columbia River), Ashley Parsons (Kazakhstan), Sarah Reid (Vanuatu), Brendan Sainsbury (Curitiba; Edmonton), Regis St. Louis (Lowcountry & Coastal Georgia), Maria Stayanova (Bansko), Oliver Smith (Jordan Trail), Aydan Stuart (Chiang Mai; Laos), Nicola Williams (Lithuania; Toulouse; Valais)

Printed in Malaysia

ISBN 9781837582990

© Lonely Planet 2024

© photographers as indicated 2024

Front cover photos © Justin Foulkes/Lonely Planet; Roberto Lo Savio/Shutterstock; Maya Karkalicheva/Getty Images; Jacob Kupferman/Getty Images; Nikita Melnichenko/ Alamy Stock Photo.

Back cover photos © chanchai duangdoosan/Shutterstock; Sophie Dover/iStock; Stefano Politi Markovina/Shutterstock.

Map data:

© Lonely Planet

© OpenStreetMap contributors

© Natural Earth

NASA/METI/AIST/Japan Spacesystems, and U.S./Japan ASTER Science Team (2019). ASTER Global Digital Elevation Model V003.

https://data.humdata.org/dataset/cod-ab-jpn?

https://fastestknowntime.com/route/jordan-trail-jordan

https://listdata.thelist.tas.gov.au/opendata/index.html#LIST_ Land_Districts

https://www.geoportal.sk/en/zbgis/download/

Lonely Planet Global Limited

Digital Depot, Roe Lane (off Thomas St),
Digital Hub, Dublin 8, D08 TCV4 Ireland

STAY IN TOUCH
lonelyplanet.com/contact